Book of Wonders of the World

BPI INDIA PVT LTD

EAN: 978817693714-6

Published by

BPI INDIA PVT LTD

16, Ansari Road, Darya Ganj,
New Delhi-110002
Tel: 2328 4898, 2327 6118 Fax: 2327 1653
email: bpipl@vsnl.com, bpiindia@airtelbroadband.in

Contributions:
Editors: C.V. Indira, Kathakoli Dasgupta, Rituparna Sengupta, D.Satya
Design: Vidya Saxena, Amit Singh, Shiv Shankar Sharma, Anoop Bishwas
Production: Sudhakar Mishra

Printed by Gopsons

Contents

Wonders of the World

Great Pyramid at Giza

The only surviving wonder of the ancient world, the Great Pyramid, is located at Giza, which is now a part of Greater Cairo, Egypt. It is the largest of the three pyramids at Giza, Necropolis. The Great Pyramid was built as a tomb for the Pharaoh Khufu.

Ancient Egyptians believed that their pharaoh was divine. He was seen as the Egyptians' representative to the gods. The Egyptians buried their pharaoh in a tomb with all his earthly belongings. The funeral was an elaborate affair where the pharaoh's body was mummified and made ready for his afterlife journey to heaven.

Khufu's pyramid

From about 2600 B.C., the Egyptians began building pyramids, as tombs for their pharaohs. The Great Pyramid was the largest and the most famous of these pyramids. It was built between 2589-2566 B.C. The Great Pyramid is also known as Khufu's pyramid or the Pyramid of Khufu.

Construction of Pyramid

Three chambers

Inside the Great Pyramid there are three chambers. These chambers are known as the "King's chamber", "Queen's chamber" and "Underground chamber". The "King's chamber" was the burial chamber of Pharaoh Khufu. The "Queen's chamber" was not a burial chamber for Khufu's queen. It was probably built as a room to hold Khufu's funerary objects. The "Underground chamber" was the largest chamber and was 27.4 m below the ground level. No one is quite sure why this chamber was built. It was probably left unfinished for religious reasons or was built to fool robbers and lead them away from the real burial chamber.

Construction

Historians and archaeologists believe that it took about 20 years to build the Great Pyramid. Most of the 100,000 workers were farmers, who worked during the flood season when their fields were underwater. The Great Pyramid was built of about two million blocks of stone, each weighing more than two tonnes.

Construction theories

Over the years, several theories have been proposed regarding the construction of the Great Pyramid. According to one theory of construction, a straight or spiral ramp coated with mud and water was raised around the pyramid, which was used to haul up the huge stone blocks. According to another theory, the blocks were placed using long levers with a short angled foot.

Tallest structure

The Great Pyramid was the tallest structure on Earth for more than 43 centuries until the Eiffel tower was built in 1889. The Great Pyramid was made of granite and limestone, and stood at a height of about 147 m after its completion. It is now 138 m high. The base of the Pyramid covers an area of about 52.813 sq km. The length of each side was originally 229.8 m, but now measures 227 m. The sloping angle of its sides is 54° 54′. The total mass of the pyramid is around 6 million tonnes.

Architect

The Great Pyramid was designed by the architect Hemon. Hemon was a vizier or advisor in Pharaoh Khufu's court.

Hanging Gardens of Babylon

The Hanging Gardens of Babylon were one of the Seven Wonders of the Ancient World. The gardens were built by King Nebuchadnezzar II. Nebuchadnezzar II ruled Babylon from 605 to 562 B.C. The Hanging Gardens do not exist today.

The Hanging Gardens of Babylon were located on the east bank of the River Euphrates, about 48 km south of Baghdad, Iraq. It was covered with trees, flowers, lawns, plants, fountains, pools, and miniature waterfalls. In reality, the gardens did not hang, but grew on the roofs and terraces of the royal palace in Babylon.

Artist's imagination of the Hanging Gardens of Babylon

History

King Nebuchadnezzar II built the gardens of Babylon for Amytis, his Median wife. Amytis came from a place where there were mountainous plains all around, and in the barren lands of Mesopotamia, she missed the greenery of her homeland. Nebuchadnezzar II wanted to recreate Amytis' homeland for her. He built a terrace garden using mud, sun-dried bricks and stone. Ox-carts and river barges were used to carry plants and trees to the gardens. Each level had flowers, trees, and other plants and the garden almost looked like a real mountain.

Babylon

Babylon was an ancient city in Mesopotamia. It was the capital of Babylonia in the 2nd and 1st millennia B.C. The ruins of Babylon can be found east of Euphrates, about 88.5 km south of Baghdad, in present day Iraq. The name Babylon means "gate of god."

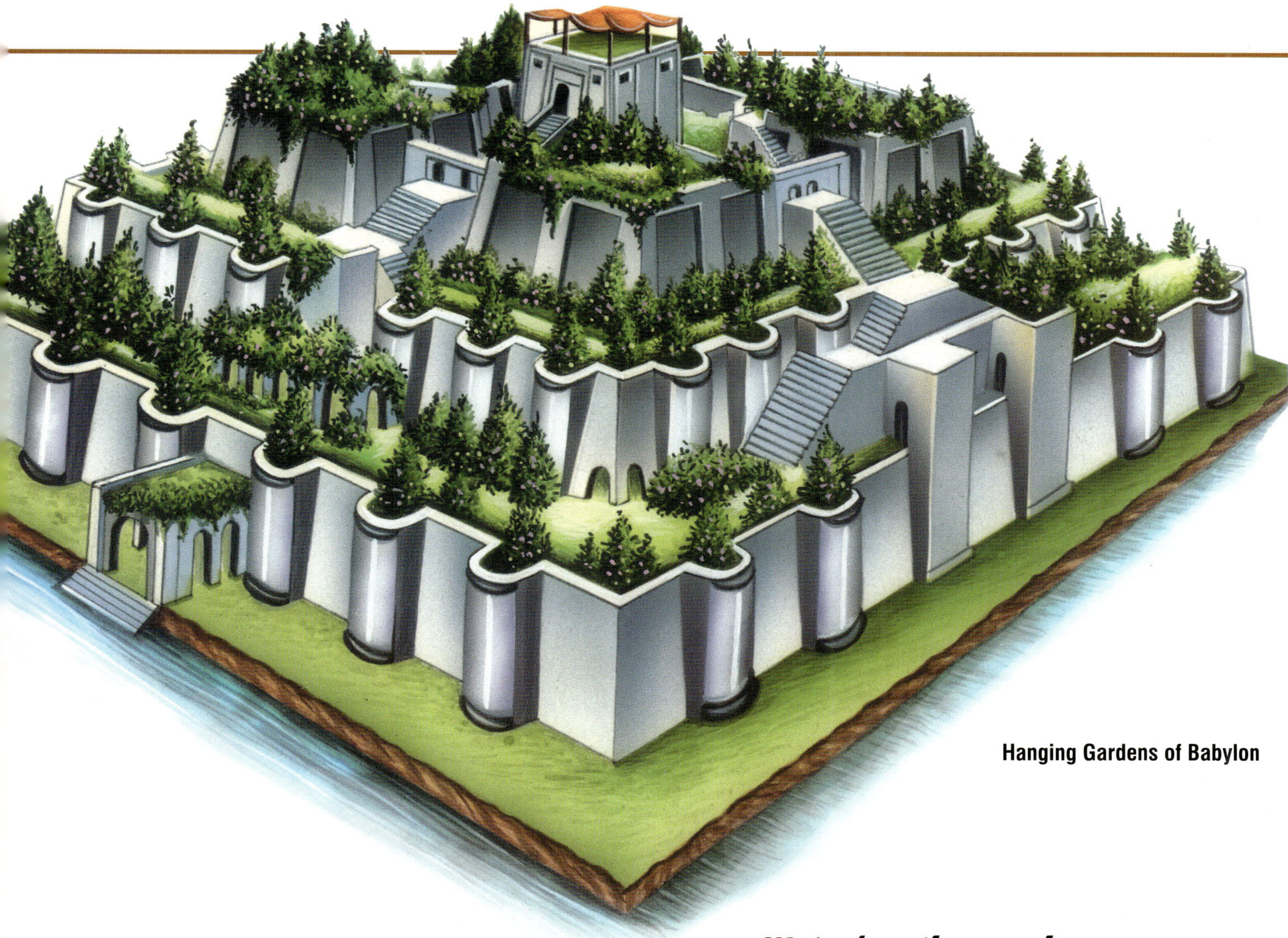

Hanging Gardens of Babylon

Nebuchadnezzar, the Great

King Nebuchadnezzar II was a ruler of the Chaldean dynasty. He was the most important king of Babylon. Nebuchadnezzar II proved to be one of the mightiest kings of his time and was often called "Nebuchadnezzar, the Great." He marched his troops against Egypt and defeated them in the battle of Carchemish, in present day Syria. He also invaded many cities, restored several old religious monuments, and improved canals. Nebuchadnezzar is best known for his Hanging Gardens in Babylon as well as for the Ishtar Gate.

Watering the garden

Babylon was a dry and barren desert land. Once Nebuchadnezzar built the garden and planted the trees and plants to make his Queen happy, he was faced with the problem of watering it. The only major water source in the city was the river Euphrates. But transporting water from the river bank to the high terrace garden was not an easy task. The King employed prisoners of war to water the gardens. It is assumed by historians that probably a chain pump system was used to lift water to the various levels of the terrace garden. The pump had two large wheels, one above the other, connected by a chain. Buckets hung on the connected chain and as the wheels turned, the buckets would go down and get filled with water. The water in the bucket was then poured in a pool at the top. The empty buckets were then taken back and the cycle continued. Without the use of the chain pump the Hanging Gardens of Babylon would have never flourished. Besides, the chain pump system, other technologies were also used during the construction of the gardens.

Temple of Artemis

Temple of Artemis

The Temple of Artemis was one of the Seven Wonders of the Ancient World. It was located in the ancient city of Ephesus, near the modern town of Selcuk, in Turkey.

The temple was built around 550 B.C. in honour of the Greek goddess Artemis. Artemis was the goddess of hunting who protected wild animals. It was believed that she roamed through the woods with a band of women comrades. For the Greeks, Artemis was also the goddess of the Moon. The Temple of Artemis took 120 years to build. It was one of the largest temples ever built in ancient times. The temple was used both as a marketplace and as a religious centre. Kings, merchants, pilgrims, artisans, and tourists visited the temple and offered gifts to Artemis. Gifts included statuettes of Artemis made of gold and ivory, earrings, bracelets and necklaces. The temple also had artifacts from the faraway lands of Persia and India.

Structure

The temple had a magnificent statue of the goddess Artemis. It was made of gold, ebony, silver and black stone. The temple also had several other works of art. These included four bronze statues of Amazon women, and a sacred stone. The stone was believed to have fallen from Jupiter. It was probably a meteorite that had fallen from the sky. The temple was made entirely of marble and had a tile covered wooden roof. It had a decorated facade overlooking a spacious courtyard. The temple was rectangular. Its foundation was about 130 m long and about 68 m wide. The temple had around 127 columns that supported the roof. The carved circular columns were about 20 m high. The temple was surrounded by marble steps that led to a platform or high terrace.

Architects

The temple was designed by the Greek architect Chersiphron, his son Metagenes, and Theodoros.

History

The temple of Artemis was built and destroyed several times by various kings and invaders. Croesus, the king of Lydia built the temple for the first time in 550 B.C. It was burned down by Herostratus in 356 B.C. to immortalize his name in history. The temple was rebuilt in the next twenty years. This time, the temple was given a higher base and decorated by Scopas and Apelles. Scopas was a Greek sculptor and architect, and Apelles was a famous painter of Ancient Greece. In 333 B.C., when Alexander, the Great came to Ephesus the temple was still under construction. Alexander wanted to help rebuild the destroyed temple but the Greeks did not accept his offer. In 262 A.D., the temple was once again destroyed by the Goths. The Ephesians took a vow to rebuild it again. It took them many years to do so. The Temple of Artemis was finally completely destroyed by St. John Chrysostom in 401 A.D. Ephesus was later deserted and no one ever again tried to build the temple.

Scene outside the Temple of Artemis

Pillars of the temple

Statue of Zeus at Olympia

The Statue of Zeus were one of the Seven Wonders of the Ancient World. It was located in the ancient town of Olympia, inside the temple of Zeus.

The Olympic Games were one of the most important festivals of the Greeks. The games were held in honour of the King of their gods, Zeus. During the games, a hundred cattle were sacrificed in the temple. The Olympic Games were first started in 776 B.C. It was held at a shrine of Zeus. Athletes from Asia Minor, Syria, Egypt and Sicily went there to compete in the games. The games, held every four years, helped to unify the Greek city-states. Initially, the site consisted of a stadium and a sacred grove or Altis. The temples were located at the Altis. But as the games became popular the need for a larger temple was felt. A new larger temple was built for Zeus, the King of gods. The construction started between 470 and 460 B.C. and the temple was completed around 456 B.C.

The architects

The Temple of Zeus was designed by Libon of Elis. The Statue of Zeus was built around 430 B.C. after the temple was constructed. The statue was carved by Phidias. Phidias was considered the greatest of all Greek sculptors. He began working on the statue around 440 B.C. It took almost eight years to build the huge statue.

The Statue of Zeus inside the Temple of Zeus

Structure

The temple of Zeus was over 64 m long and 18 m high. There were 13 large columns on both sides of the temple and 6 columns on the front and back. These columns supported a white marble roof. The exterior of the temple was painted and ornately decorated with sculptures depicting scenes from Greek mythology. The interior, however, was simple and plain. The Statue of Zeus was inside the temple. It was made of ivory and gold. The statue was as high as a modern four-storied building. The head of Zeus almost touched the ceiling. It stood at a height of about 12 m. The base of the statue was 6 m wide and about 1 m high. The statue was seated on a throne that was decorated with gold, ebony, ivory, and precious stones. The face of the statue was made of ivory. The eyes were made of precious gems. The hair, beard, sandals, and robe were made of gold. Zeus had a statue of Nike, the goddess of victory, in his right hand and a scepter with an eagle on top, in his left hand. He also had an olive wreath on his head.

Archeological findings

In 1829, a group of French scientists searched Olympia site for the first time. There found the outlines of the temple. The next expedition was by a group of German scientists. They began their expedition in 1875 and worked for the next five summers.

History

The Statue of Zeus lost its importance after Emperor Theodosius I of Rome abolished the Olympic Games. He ordered the temple of Zeus to be shut down. After about 391 A.D. the statue was carried away by wealthy Greeks to a palace in Constantinople. There it was destroyed by a fire in 462 A.D. The temple of Zeus was also damaged by fire in the 5th century A.D.

Mausoleum at Halicarnassus

The huge Mausoleum at Halicarnassus was one of the Seven Wonders of the Ancient World. It was situated in the city of Bodrum on the Aegean Sea, in southwest Turkey.

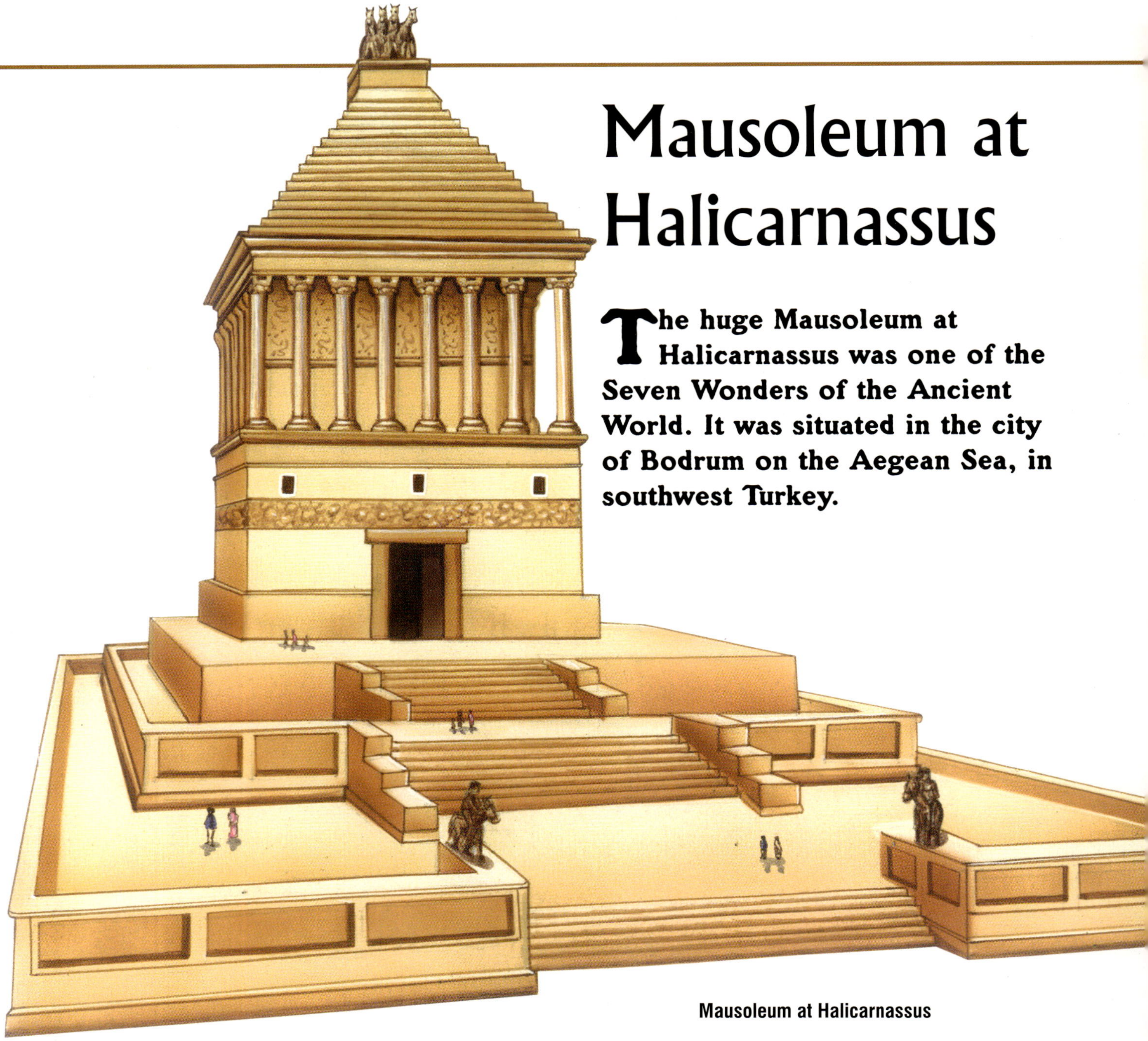

Mausoleum at Halicarnassus

The Mausoleum at Halicarnassus was the tomb of King Mausollos of Caria. Mausollos, with his sister and queen Artemisia, ruled over Halicarnassus for 24 years. Mausollos was an admirer of the Greek way of life and government. He founded many cities modelled on the Greek cities along the coast and also encouraged Greek democratic traditions. The Mausoleum was built by queen Artemisia. The construction started during Mausollos's lifetime. It was completed around 350 B.C., three years after his death. Queen Artemisia too died a year before the mausoleum was completed.

History of destruction

The mausoleum overlooked the city of Halicarnassus for many centuries. It stood above the city ruins for some 16 centuries until a series of earthquakes destroyed the columns and brought down the stone chariot to the ground. In the 15th century, Halicarnassus was invaded by the Knights of St. John of Malta. They used the marble and stone of the mausoleum to build a crusader castle. By 1404 A.D, just the base of the mausoleum was left. The broken stones of the great mausoleum were later used by people to build their own buildings.

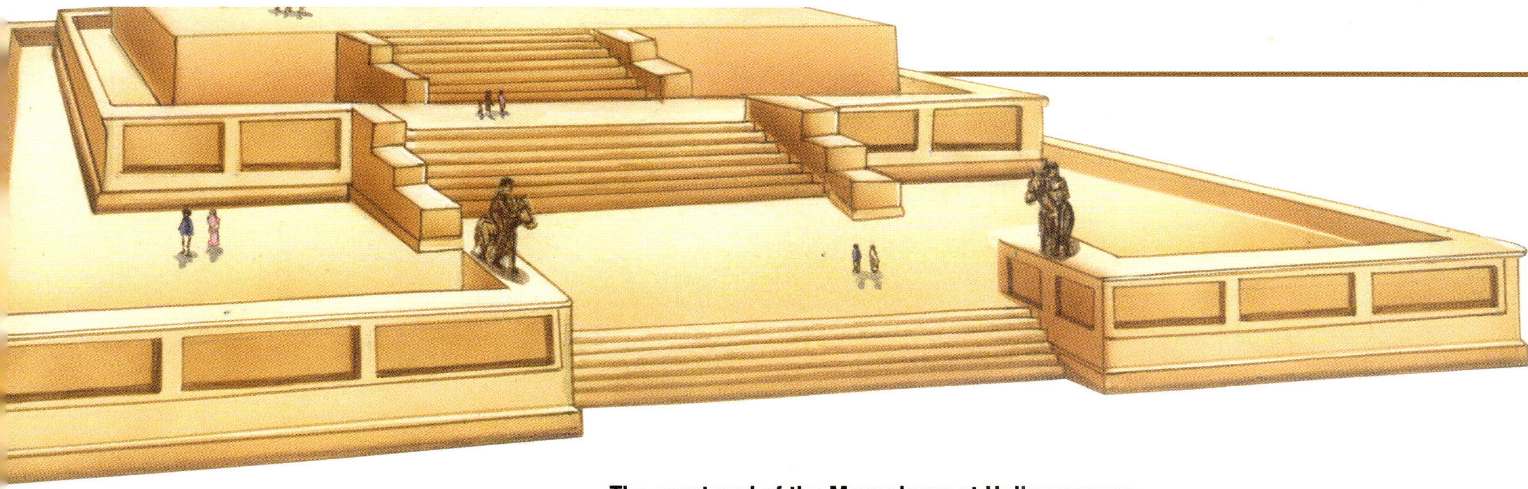

The courtyard of the Mausoleum at Halicarnassus

Structure

The Mausoleum at Halicarnassus was constructed in an enclosed courtyard on a hill overlooking the city. It had a rectangular-shaped base that was 37 m long and 30 m wide and 43 m high. The building was divided into a podium that was 18 m high, a colonnade (12 m high), and a pyramid (7 m high). The walls of the mausoleum were decorated with statues and carvings of human figures and the four sides of the tomb were decorated with battle scenes. The whole place was also decorated with life-size carvings of animal figures. A staircase, flanked by stone lions, led to the top of the podium. The burial chamber and the tomb were at the centre of the podium. Marble and stone warriors, mounted on horseback guarded the corners of the mausoleum. At the top of the mausoleum, stood a statue of a chariot pulled by four horses with Mausollos and Artemisia riding in it.

Archeological findings

In 1846, Charles Thomas Newton, an archeologist, went in search of the remains of the Mausoleum at Halicarnassus. Newton was able to locate a few walls, a staircase, and three corners of the foundation. He excavated the site and found sections of a decorated wall and portions of the roof. He also found a broken stone chariot wheel that was around 2 m in diameter. Finally, he found the statues of Mausollos and Artemisia that had stood at the summit of the Mausoleum.

Architects

The Mausoleum at Halicarnassus was designed by the architect Pythius. The four sides were sculpted by four famous sculptors of the time, Scopas, Bryaxis, Leochares, and Timotheus.

The main mausoleum

Colossus of Rhodes

The Colossus of Rhodes was one of the Seven Wonders of the Ancient World. Built at the entrance to the harbor of the Mediterranean island of Rhodes in Greece, the Colossus was the tallest statue of the ancient world.

The statue of Colossus was built in honor of the Sun God Helios, after the island of Rhodes survived a siege by the Antigonids of Macedonia in 304 B.C. The Macedonians attacked Rhodes but they failed to penetrate the city and finally went back leaving behind their supplies and equipment. The Rhodians sold the supplies and used the money to build the Colossus and celebrate their victory. The construction of the statue started immediately after the Macedonian attack and was completed after twelve years, in 282 B.C.

Architect

The Colossus was built by a Rhodian sculptor, Chares of Lindos. Chares was a patriot, who had fought to defend the city. He was a student of Lysippos, who was considered one of the greatest sculptors of the Classical Greek era. Before he started making the Colossus, Chares made smaller versions of it, which helped him later to build the great statue. It is believed that Chares died before the completion of the Colossus.

Structure

The Colossus was built using white marble, bronze, iron and stone. The statue was about 33.5 m tall and stood upon a 15 m high pedestal near the harbor. Chares used bronze plates to build the exterior of the statue and white marble for the base. The plates were carefully shaped and then raised to the right position on the figure. Iron was used for the statue's framework, and stone columns supported it. These columns were connected to the outer skin with iron beams that were driven into the stone. It is estimated that around 13,600 kg of bronze, and 8160 kg of iron were used to make the Colossus. Most of the bronze used in the statue was obtained by melting the war machines left behind by the Macedonians. People over the ages have imagined the statue of Colossus in different ways. It has been popularly depicted with its legs spanning the harbour entrance, and ships passing beneath it. It has also been thought to be more like other Greek statues: nude and holding a cloak in the left hand.

Colossus of Rhodes

Entrance to the harbour

Destruction

The Colossus of Rhodes stood for 56 years at the harbor entrance until it was struck down by an earthquake that hit Rhodes around 226 B.C. The Egyptian king, Ptolemy III offered to have the great statue reconstructed, but the Rhodians refused to rebuild it. They believed that they had offended the Sun God in some way and hence the statue was destroyed. The remains of the great statue lay on the ground for almost 800 years. In the middle of the 7th century, when the Arabs conquered Rhodes they broke the remains of the Colossus into smaller pieces and sold them as scrap metal.

The Statue of Liberty and the Colossus

Colossus and the Statue of Liberty

The Colossus has inspired many modern sculptors and their works. One of the best examples is the French sculptor Auguste Bartholdi's famous work—The Statue of Liberty. The Statue of Liberty and the Colossus are roughly of the same size and have a similar framework. The Colossus had bronze plates over an iron framework while the Statue of Liberty has an almost similar framework of steel with copper plates over it.

Pharos of Alexandria

The Pharos or Lighthouse of Alexandria was one of the Seven Wonders of the Ancient World. It was located on the island of Pharos in the harbour of Alexandria, Egypt.

The Pharos was built in the 3rd century B.C. Its construction was intiated by Ptolemy Soter, a commander of Alexander the Great in 290 B.C. Soter did not live to see the Lighthouse completed. His son Ptolemy Philadelphus completed it and dedicated the Lighthouse to Ptolemy Soter and his wife Berenice. The Pharos was built to guide ships safely to the harbour of Alexandria. It was the first Lighthouse in the world and the last of the ancient wonders to be destroyed (around 1480 A.D.).

An old depiction of the Pharos

The Lighthouse of Alexandria

Structure

Scientists have estimated the Pharos to have been almost 117 m tall. It was almost equivalent to a modern day 40-storey building. The construction of the great lighthouse happened in three stages. The lowest segment of the Pharos was around 55.9 m high. The middle segment was octagonal in shape. It was 18 m wide and 27 m high. The third segment was circular and it was 7.3 m high. A long vaulted ramp led to the entrance of the lighthouse and a spiral staircase led up to the chambers above. The stairs were used to carry fuel to the top, where fire burned at night to show the way to the harbor. During the day a mirror at the top reflected sunlight and guided the ships ashore.

History

The Pharos stood for almost seventeen centuries until it was destroyed by two strong earthquakes in the 14th century. On 8 August 1303, a violent earthquake shook the eastern Mediterranean basin and destroyed the lighthouse to a great extent. It was struck by another strong earthquake in 1323 and the lighthouse collapsed in 1326.
In 1480, Sultan Qaitbayan, an Egyptian Sultan, decided to build an Islamic fortress to strenghten the defense of Alexandria. He built the fort on the same spot, where once the great lighthouse stood. Sultan Qaitbayan used the fallen stone and marble of the Lighthouse to build the fort.

Archeological findings

Underwater remains of the Pharos have been located in the Alexandrian harbour by archeologists. These remains have been located in the recent past using the modern technology of remote imaging.

The architect

The Pharos was designed by the Greek architect and engineer Sostratus of Cnidus.

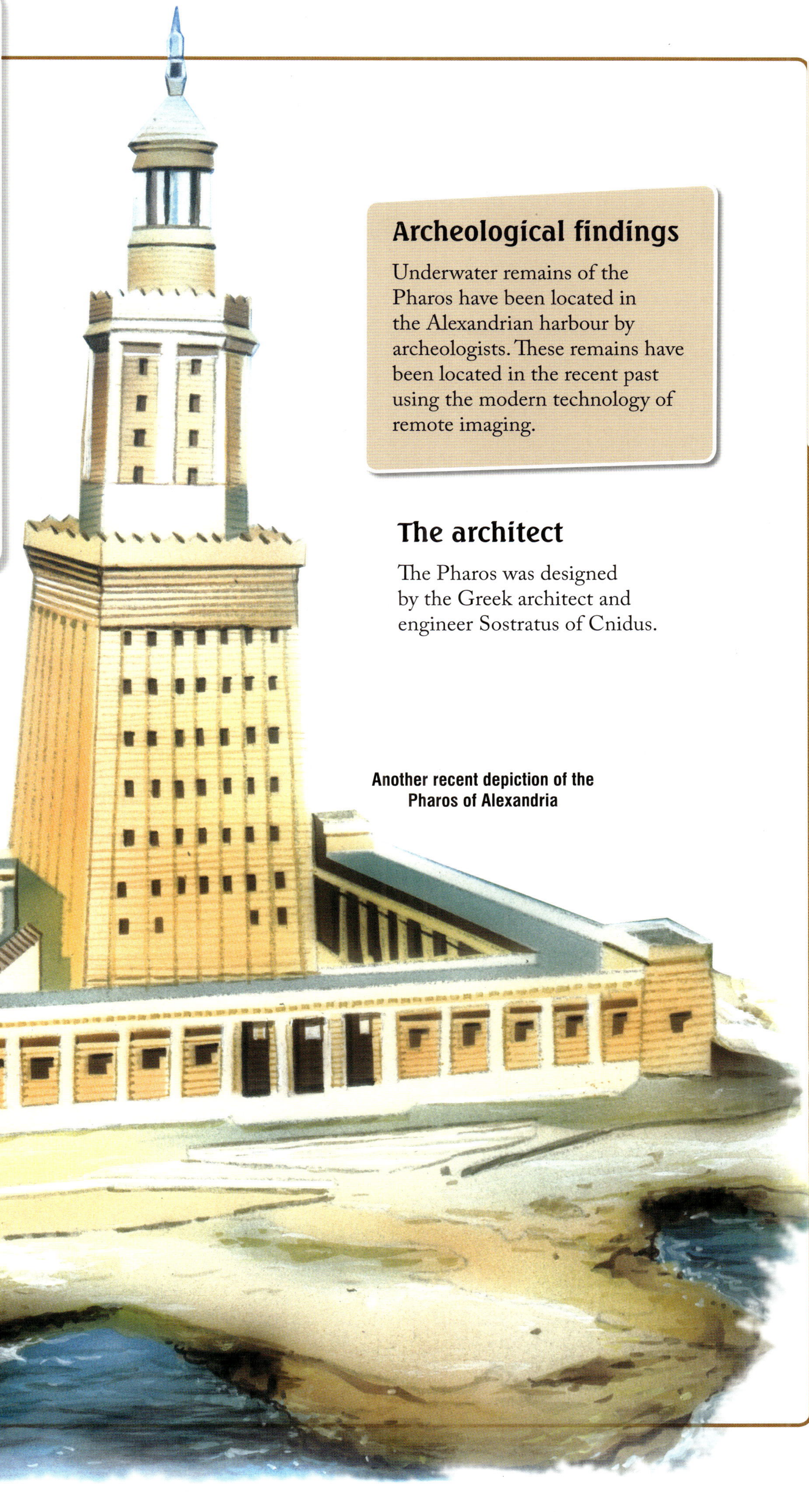

Another recent depiction of the Pharos of Alexandria

Colosseum

The Colosseum of Rome was the greatest theater of ancient times. Built in Rome by the Flavian Roman emperors, the Colosseum is one of the finest examples of Roman architecture.

The construction of the Colosseum was initiated by Emperor Vespasian between 70 and 76 A.D and was completed a year after his death by his son Titus in 80 A.D.

History

In 64 A.D., Nero the Emperor of Rome built a huge pleasure palace for himself right in the center of the city. He called it the Golden House. But Nero could not enjoy the pleasures of the palace for many years. After a military uprising in 68 A.D., Nero committed suicide leaving the Roman empire engulfed in civil wars. Titus Flavius Vespasianus emerged as the winner and founded the Flavian dynasty. He was known as the Roman Emperor Vespasian. Titus ruled Rome from 69 to 79 A.D. During his rule, he decided to build an amphitheater or place of pleasure for the people of Rome on the site of the lake in the gardens of Nero's palace. This amphitheater was the Colosseum. The Colosseum was so named because it was built near the place, where Nero had erected a huge statue or colossus of himself.

Structure

Almost every sports stadium in the world today follows the basic design of the Colosseum. The Colosseum was an elliptical building with four stories. It had a circumference of 527 m and was about 48 m high. Around 100,000 cubic metres of marble, and 300 tonnes of iron were used to build the great amphitheatre. Many materials—tufa, a form of limestone, travertine, a sedimentary rock, and bricks—were used in the construction of the Colosseum. The inner part of the Colosseum was divided into the arena, podium, and cavea. The ramped seating area was made of concrete and the floors were wooden with open chambers beneath. There were 80 entrances to the amphitheater of which four were reserved for the Emperor, other VIPs and gladiators. The Colosseum was decorated by Greek columns on the outside.

The roof of the Colosseum was a huge canvas that was stretched using a system of ropes and pulleys by a specially trained team of Roman sailors. The canvas had a large hole in the center to admit light into the amphitheater.

The outer wall of the Colosseum

Colosseum

Sports and Entertainment

The Colosseum was built to entertain Roman citizens. To celebrate the opening of the great amphitheater, games were held for around 100 days. Lavish theatrical productions, tamed animal acts, bloody contests pitting gladiators against gladiators, and wild beasts were some of the favourite sports and pastimes of the Romans. The Colosseum proved to be the perfect place to stage all these sporting events, especially because thousands of people could watch and cheer together here. The infamous gladiator fight was the most popular sport. The gladiators were generally slaves, prisoners of war or criminals. Other popular sports included bullfights, fights between wild animals, and men and tamed beasts.

Destruction

The Colosseum was used for almost 500 years. It was then badly damaged by a series of earthquakes. The damaged Colosseum became a source of building materials for various other buildings. Pope Paul III used the Colosseum's stones to build his own palace. Today what we see of the Colosseum is just one-third of the great architecture. The last games at the Colosseum were held in the 6th century A.D.

Inside the Colosseum

Great Wall of China

The Great Wall of China is one of the Wonders of the World. The Great Wall is not a single wall but a series of walls built and rebuilt by different Chinese dynasties over a thousand years. The Great Wall stretches to about 6560 km from East to West of China. It is the largest man-made structure on Earth.

The construction of the Great Wall was conceived over 2000 years ago by Qin Shi Huangdi, the first Emperor of China. He was the founder of the Qin (Ch'in) Dynasty that ruled China from 221 B.C. – 206 B.C. Shi Huangdi decided to construct a great wall by unifying all the independent walls built in ancient times to protect China from the raids of the northern nomadic tribes. The Great Wall became the world's greatest military structure during the Ming dynasty.

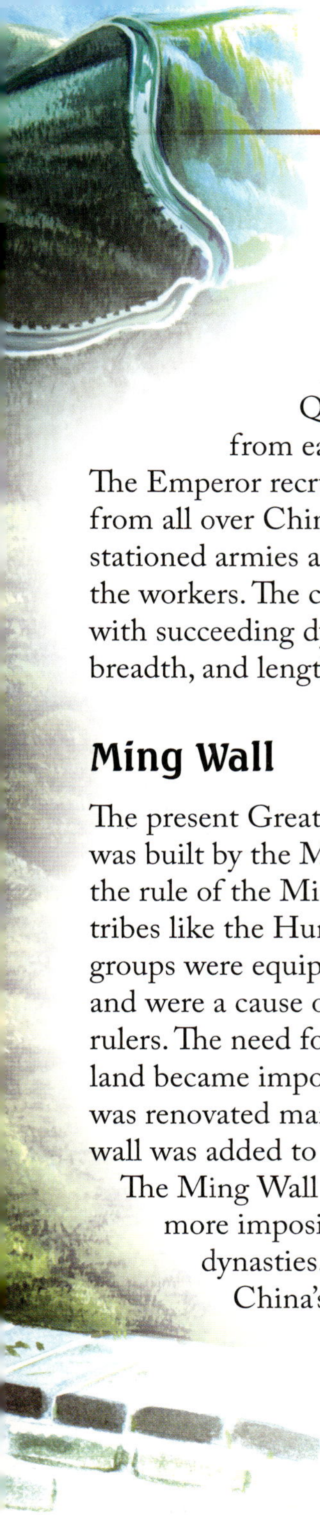

The first wall

The first walls were constructed between the 7th and 8th centuries B.C. by Emperor Shi Huangdi of the Qin Dynasty. This wall stretched from east to west for about 4960 km. The Emperor recruited peasants and prisoners from all over China to build the wall. He stationed armies at the wall to stand guard over the workers. The construction lasted for centuries with succeeding dynasties adding to the height, breadth, and length of the wall.

Ming Wall

The present Great Wall, which we are familiar with, was built by the Ming dynasty (1368–1644). During the rule of the Ming dynasty, the northern nomadic tribes like the Huns became very powerful. The groups were equipped with modern ammunitions and were a cause of constant threat to the Ming rulers. The need for a stronger wall to protect their land became important. During this period, the Wall was renovated many times and another 960 km long wall was added to the existing wall.

The Ming Wall was bigger, longer, and more imposing than the walls of the previous dynasties. The wall passed through some of China's most hostile landscapes.

Dimensions

The Great Wall stands at a height of 7.5 m. The base of the wall is around 7.5 m thick but it narrows down to 4.5 m at the top. Guard stations and watchtowers are placed at regular intervals along the length of the wall.

Smoke signals

The Chinese troops and workers used smoke by day to send messages along the length of the Great Wall. They burnt wood and straw mixed with wolf dung, which produced rich black columns of smoke. There were different types of signals for different situations. For instance, a one-column smoke indicated an impending attack by a force of less than 500 men and a two-column smoke indicated that there was a force of less than 3000 men. A four column smoke signal meant a force of 10,000 men.

Materials used

The Great Wall was built of stone, wood, grass and earth. The Mings used advanced brick building technology and had state-of-the-art kilns to mass-produce bricks, which were as strong as modern-day masonry blocks. In many places, a mixture of sticky rice and egg whites was used to cement the stones or bricks together. The bricks were transported by men, donkeys, mules, and goats. There were areas where the wall passed through deserts or barren lands. In those portions, it was constructed using dirt rammed between rough woods and tied together with woven mats.

General Meng Tian

General Meng Tian supervised the construction of the Great Wall for the first time. According to historians, the general mobilised 300,000 labourers for the construction of the Great Wall during the Qin dynasty.

The Great Wall and the watch towers

Maya Temples

Some of the most beautiful and elaborate temples in the world were built by the Maya. The temples were built on immense pyramids with stepped bases. Each side of the pyramid had a set of steps that led up to the temple.

The Mayan civilization was one of the most advanced civilizations of Central America. It was established around 1500 B.C. and thrived for 2000 years. The Maya had their own fully developed written language, spectacular art, and monumental architecture. They had also developed a sophisticated mathematical and astronomical system. Some Maya centers like Chichen Itza, Uxmal, and Mayapan flourished for several centuries.

Pyramid temple at Chichen Itza

Religion

Religion was an important part of Mayan a life. It ruled almost everything in the life of the Mayans. Priests were considered one of the most important people in Mayan society. They were usually the ruling chiefs. The Mayans believed that their gods had destroyed and recreated the Earth several times. So they always tried to please their gods with sacrifices. Most Mayan a gods were related to nature and were referred to as a god of some part of nature. Their Supreme Being was Hunan Ku, who was also considered the creator of the

Pyramid-temples

The Maya temples usually had a number of pyramid-type mounds with the main temple at the top. Some of the pyramid-temples were tall and steep, some very broad, while others were squat. The temples were built out of beautifully carved stones. The exterior was adorned with elaborate stucco decorations and the interior was decorated with mural paintings. The temple had a single floor, which generally comprised of one to three dark rooms and an inner chamber, where the king performed his rituals.

Chichen Itza

Chichen Itza was an important Mayan city. It is one of the most important archaeological sites of the Mayan civilization exhibiting a multitude of architectural styles. The city had splendid architectural masterpieces like the Temple of Chac Mool, the Hall of Thousand Pillars, the Playing Field of the Prisoners and the Temple of Kukulcan.

Temple of the warriors

Temple of the Warriors

The Temple of the Warriors at Chichen Itza is a large step-pyramid fronted and flanked by rows of carved columns depicting warriors. At the top of the stairway on the pyramid's summit that leads toward the entrance of the temple is a chac mool. The chac mool was an altar where offerings to the gods were placed.

High Priest's Temple

The High Priest's Temple at Chichen Itza is a step-pyramid temple. It is a smaller version of the Temple of Kukulcan. The temple was actually a tomb for one of the city's rulers.

Temple of Kukulcan

The Temple of Kukulcan or El Castillo was located at the center of Chichen Itza. It was one of the most important temples at Chichen Itza. The temple is a step-pyramid with stairways on all four sides leading to a temple at the top. In fact, there are two temples on the pyramid. The Maya is built a larger and grander temple atop the older temple. Inside the older temple, one can still see King Kukulcan's Jaguar throne, carved of stone and painted red with jade spots. The pyramid of Kukulcan was the last Maya temple to be built.

Temples at Tikal

Tikal is the largest of the ancient ruined cities of the Mayan civilization. It is located in the rainforests of Guatemala. The most prominent buildings among the ruins are the six Mesoamerican step-pyramid temples known as Temples I—VI. Most of these pyramid temples were built between the late 7th and early 9th century A.D.

Pyramid temple at Tikal

Tikal Temple I

Tikal Temple I, also known as Temple of the Giant Jaguar or the Temple of Ah Cacao, is one of the major structures at Tikal. Built around 695 A.D., the temple is located in the Petén Basin region of northern Guatemala. The temple is a step-pyramid with a height of approximately 44 m. The main chamber of the temple depicts Kukulcan, a feathered serpent god. The temple also houses the tomb of Jasaw Chan K'awiil I, a Classicera ruler of the Mayan civilization.

Pyramid temple at Uxmal

Temples at Uxmal

Uxmal is one of the most well known cities of the Mayan civilization. The Adivino or Pyramid of the Magician is the most famous pyramid temple at Uxmal.

Mayan calendar

The Maya had a highly sophisticated calendar system and hieroglyphic writing. In Chichen Itza, at El Castillo, a Maya calendar is set in stone, with 365 steps representing the days of the year.

Machu Picchu

Machu Picchu is an ancient Inca city built on top of a high mountain. It lies hidden and completely invisible from below. It is located in the Urubamba Valley, in the Andes Mountains of Peru. The valley was known as the Sacred Valley of the Incas.

The name Machu Picchu, in Quechua language means "Old Mountain". Machu Picchu was built between 1460 and 1470 A.D. by Pachacuti Inca Yupanqui, an Inca ruler. Located at an altitude of 2430 m above sea level, Machu Picchu was most likely a royal estate and a religious retreat.

Mount Picchu

Cultivation

Cultivation was the primary occupation of many people at Machu Picchu. Potatoes and maize were two crops that were cultivated by the Incas. They used advanced terracing and irrigation methods to reduce soil erosion and increase the area available for cultivation to get the highest possible yield.

Decline

The existence of Machu Picchu was not known to many outside the Incas. The city declined after 1527 A.D., when fifty percent of the population was killed by small pox. Much of the place fell into disuse after the Spanish arrived in the Cuzco Valley in 1533 A.D. and not long after the city was swallowed up by the jungles.

Architecture

The city of Machu Picchu was surrounded by high mountain peaks and rushing waters. It was divided into two large sectors—the urban sector and the agricultural sector. The urban sector had plazas, platforms, and about 200 buildings. A system of narrow lanes or paths connected the platforms. Most of the buildings were residences and the rest few included temples, storage structures and other public buildings. The storage structures were carved out of gray granite and were filled with magnificent treasures. Houses in the city were constructed in groups of ten around a communal courtyard. They were aligned on narrow terraces and were connected by narrow alleys. At the center of a group of houses, was a large open square that was used as a livestock enclosure. Most of the houses were two storied with steep thatched roofs and trapezoidal doors. They were built of stone and granite blocks that were fitted together without mortar.

Hiram Bingham III

The lost city of Machu Picchu was discovered by American archaeologist and politician Hiram Bingham III in 1911. Bingham removed the overgrown vegetation and discovered the ruins of the city in a remote part of the Peruvian Andes.

Population

Machu Picchu had a population of almost 1200 people. Most of the residents were women, children and priests. The Inca rulers and their families spent a few weeks or months at the city. Most of the people who lived there permanently were the servants of the Inca rulers. A small percentage of the population consisted of metalworkers and specialized craftspeople.

Astronomical observatory

The city of Machu Picchu served as an astronomical observatory to the Incas. The Intihuatana stone found at Machu Picchu was an indicator of the date of the two equinoxes and other significant celestial periods. On 21st March and 21st September, when the Sun is almost directly above the pillar at noon it does not create any shadow of the Intihuatana stone. The Incas believed that the Sun "sits with all his might upon the pillar" and is for a moment "tied" to the rock. The Incas considered this moment sacred and held religious ceremonies at the stone.

Stonehenge

The Stonehenge is a megalithic ruin in the Salisbury Plain in Southern England, about 128.7 km miles southwest of London. It is around 5000 years old.

The Stonehenge is not a single structure. It consists of a series of structures made of earth, timber and stone. The henge initially consisted of a circular ditch, with a raised bank on the inside. The outer circle and horseshoe of Stonehenge had 30 vertical Sarsen stones (sandstones) and an equal number of horizontal lintels. The 30 lintels rested on top of and connected the 30 upright Sarsen stones. There is another set of blue stones and Trilithons. Trilithons are ten upright stones arranged as five free-standing pairs with a single horizontal lintel. There were also four "station stones" set in a rectangle outside the ring.

Construction

The construction of the Stonehenge was done in three phases. These three phases have been labeled as Stonehenge I, II, and III by professor Richard Atkinson, a researcher at the Stonehenge.

Phase I

The first phase of the construction of the Stonehenge dates back to 2950-2900 B.C. or the Middle Neolithic age. During this phase, the Stonehenge was a circle of timbers surrounded by a ditch and bank. The circle had a diameter of 100 m. There were 56 Aubrey holes that held timber posts. The ditch was dug by hand using animal bones. Deer antlers were used as pick-axes to loosen the underlying chalk and shoulder blades of oxen or cattle were used as shovels to clear away the stones.

Stonehenge

Phase II

During the second phase, the Stonehenge was rebuilt before the arrival of the Romans in Britain. The construction started after 2900 B.C. and went on for the next 500 years until 2400 B.C.. This time blue stones were used to build the Stonehenge. These blue stones were brought from the Prescelli Mountains in Pembroke, South Wales. They were dragged down to the sea, floated on huge rafts, and brought up the River Avon to the Salisbury plains. The timber posts were no longer there and the Aubrey holes were partially filled.

Phase III

The Stonehenge was reconstructed for the third time around 2300 B.C. The reconstruction went on until 1600 B.C. During this phase the bluestones were dug up and rearranged, and placed in what are known as the Q and R Holes. Giant Sarsen stones were hammered to size and placed upright in pairs in a circle. Each pair was connected by lintels. The largest Sarsen was around 7 m in height and weighed more than 44 tonnes. The Sarsen circle was about 33 m in diameter.

During the third phase, a horseshoe-shaped arrangement of five Trilithons was also erected within the Sarsen Circle. They were arranged as five freestanding pairs each with a single horizontal lintel. The tallest Trilithon placed at the center was about 8 m tall above the ground and weighed almost 45,000 kg. The lintel placed above it weighed 9000 kg. Only three Trilithons with their lintels can be seen now.

Heel stone

The Sarsen Heel stone is a large upright boulder. It is surrounded by a circular ditch and is located along the Avenue. The stone is approximately 4.88 m in height above the ground. Another 1.22 m of the stone is buried below the ground.

Heel stone

Mystery

The construction of the Stonehenge is still a mystery. There are no records to find out why this place was built, dismantled and rebuilt over the years. Many archaeologists and historians believe that the Stonehenge was sacred ground.

Altar stone

The Altar stone lies embedded in the ground within the Trilithon Horseshoe. It is a large block of sandstone. There are two other fallen stones across it. The stone is 4.9 m long and 1 m wide. It has a thickness of 0.5 m.

Altar stone

Leaning Tower of Pisa

One of the architectural wonders of the world, the Leaning Tower, is a bell tower located in the Italian city of Pisa. The tower is about 55 m tall and has a diameter of 16 m.

The construction of the tower of Pisa began in 1173 A.D. and was completed in 1372 A.D. The tower was built to show the wealth of Pisa to the rest of the world. The people of Pisa were good sailors and conquered many lands including Jerusalem, parts of Africa, Belgium, Norway, Spain, and other places. The only enemy they had were the people of Florence, who refused to accept their greatness. So in order to show off of their wealth and power the people of Pisa started to build the bell tower and also many other buildings such as Cathedrals, Baptistery, and Cemeteries near Florence.

Bells

After the completion of the tower in 1370, seven bells were added to the tower:

- 1st bell: *L'assunta*, cast in 1654 weighing 3620 kg
- 2nd bell: *il Crocifisso*, cast in 1572 weighing 2462 kg
- 3rd bell: *San Ranieri*, cast in 1719-21 weighing 1448 kg
- 4th bell: *La Terza* (1st small one), cast in 1473, weighing 300 kg
- 5th bell: *La Pasquereccia*, cast in 1262 by Lotteringo, weighing 1014 kg
- 6th bell: *il Vespruccio* (2nd small one), cast in the fourteenth century and again in 1501 by Nicola di Jacopo, weighing 1000 kg
- 7th bell: *Del Pozzetto*, cast in 1606, weighing 652 kg

The fabulous Leaning Tower of Pisa

Construction

The great tower was not built at one go. Construction began with the base of the tower and the first foundation stones of marble and lime were set down in 1173 A.D. During the first stage, the first three floors were built. In 1178 A.D., when Pisa was at war, the construction was stopped. In 1275 A.D., construction of the next three floors was resumed again. The construction was once again halted until 1319 A.D. The final two floors were added between 1319 A.D. and 1350 A.D.

The Duomo (Cathedral) and Leaning Tower

Architect

The architect of the Leaning Tower of Pisa is a subject of controversy. Nowhere in the building and in history, is the name of the architect recorded. According to the historian Giorgio Vasari, the architect of the tower was Bonanno Pisano. According to modern historians, Diotisalvi was the architect of the tower. Diotisalvi was the architect of the Baptistery and there are similarities in the structure of the Baptistery and the tower. Some historians have attributed the design to Biduino. The ornamentation of the tower at the basement reveals noteworthy similarities with some of Biduino's most well-known work.

The lean of the Leaning Tower

Lean

The lean of the Leaning tower is because of the weak foundation and unstable subsoil. The site of the tower was a large river delta in the past. The architects and builders of the tower were however unaware of this fact. They did not know that the soil was a mixture of sand, clay and water, which was unsuitable for large buildings. The lean was noticed for the first time during the construction of the third floor in 1178 A.D. During the construction of the next three floors, the architects tried to adjust the lean. This gave the tower a slight banana shape and the tower began leaning towards south in 1272 A.D. Architects tried to correct the angle toward north by adding four steps on the north side and six steps on the south side at the base of the bell tower. This however, gave the tower a slight S-shape. Today, the tower leans about 5.5 degrees towards south.

Taj Mahal

One of the Seven Wonders of the World, the Taj Mahal, is a mausoleum built by the Mughal Emperor Shah Jahan in the memory of his beloved wife Mumtaz Mahal. Constructed entirely of pure white marble, the mausoleum is a masterpiece of Mughal architecture.

The Taj Mahal is located in India at Agra, a city about 129 km miles south of New Delhi. The Taj Mahal is a complex of many buildings. The complex is bounded on three sides by a red sandstone wall. The river Yamuna flows on the open side, acting as a moat.

Architecture

The construction of the Taj Mahal began in 1632 A.D., a year after the death of Mumtaz Mahal. The five principal elements of the complex are main gateway, garden, mosque, jawab (a building mirroring the mosque), and mausoleum (including its four minarets). The plan and design of the Taj Mahal has been attributed to various architects. It is believed that the chief architect was probably Ustad Ahmad Lahawri, an Indian of Persian descent. More than 20,000 workers took 22 years to build the 0.169 sq km Taj Mahal complex. Most of the workers were employed from India, Persia, the Ottoman Empire, and Europe. The construction of the Taj Mahal cost between four and five million rupees.

Architecture

The design of the Taj Mahal combines many of the formal themes of Islamic architecture. It is mainly based on the number four or its multiples because the number four is considered holiest in Islam. The tomb of the Taj Mahal is over 73 m high. It is decorated with Koranic inscriptions and carved relief. Apart from the main mausoleum, it has a gateway, garden, a mosque and a guesthouse. The mausoleum stands on the north side of this garden. The garden prefaces the tomb. It is 300 m wide and has a great pool at its center. The entrance to this garden is through the grand gate. The architects tried to give a best heavenly look to the monument. Two marble canals with fountains in the center of the garden divide the garden into four equal squares. This pattern is called the "charbagh plan." It was well adopted during the construction of the Taj Mahal. The garden has an elevated marble lotus pond. The water of this pond gives the perfect reflection of the great monument. The garden is irrigated by the overflowing canals. The fountains provide inlets to the north-south canal. The west-east canal received its water through an interconnection with the north-south canal.

Construction and decoration

Three types of stones were used in the construction of the Taj Mahal—semi-precious, rare and precious stones and common stones like red sandstone, yellow sandstone and white marble. These were brought from all over India and central Asia. The common sandstones were used to build the structure while the precious and semi-precious stones were used for decoration. Bricks were also used to build the skeletal structures. Various colored marbles and gemstones were used at the enhance. The Mughals believed that the precious and semiprecious stones have different effects on fortunes of different persons and places. This belief was also taken into consideration in the construction of the Taj Mahal. The architects used several methods such as carving, stucco, painting, and mosaic and inlay work to beautify this great monument. Glazed tiles were used for exterior decoration and mosaic and glass paintings were used to enhance the beauty of interiors.

The garden in front of the Taj

Angkor Wat

The main entrance to the temple

The Angkor Wat temple is located in Cambodia. It is a huge pyramid temple built during the rule of King Suryavarman II. It is regarded as the supreme masterpiece of Khmer architecture. It is the representative symbol of Cambodia and is displayed on the country's National Flag.

The temple of Angkor Wat was originally dedicated to the Hindu god Vishnu. However, later it became a shrine for Theravada Buddhists. Theravada Buddhism is the dominant religion among the contemporary Khmer people of Cambodia. The temple represents some of the most beautiful examples of Khmer and Hindu art. The temple has dominating towers, intricate carvings in the walls, and endless, courtyards and passageways outside. It is surrounded by a moat. The moat is around 173.7 m wide and about about 6.4 km long. The Angkor Wat temple is one of the greatest representations of the traditional Cambodian culture.

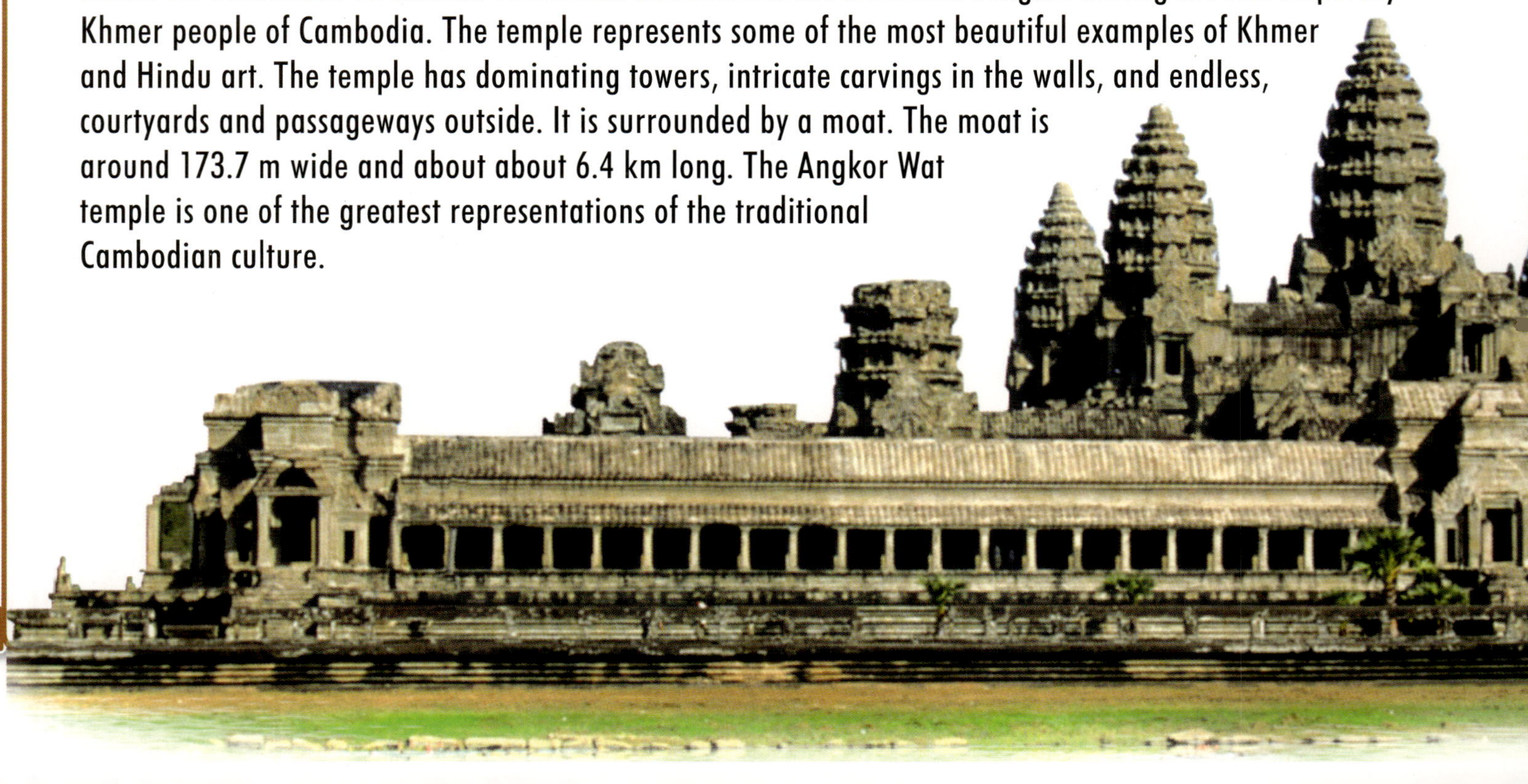

World Heritage Site

The Khmer Empire began to decline during the 13th century. It turned into a Buddhist temple with the decline. The Buddhists, maintained the temple very well and helped to preserve it. In 1989, UNESCO sent the first mission in Angkor city to assess it as a conservation site. In 1992, the UNESCO World Heritage Committee declared the Angkor city as well as the Angkor Wat temple as a World Heritage Site.

Angkor

The city of Angkor is located in northwestern Cambodia. It was founded in the early 9th century A.D. The city remained the capital city of Cambodia until the 15th century. This city has some of the most famous Indonesian temples such as the Angkor Wat Temple, the Angkor Thom Temple, and the Bayon Temple.

Architecture

The Angkor Wat temple represents the temple mountain of Mount Meru, which has great importance in Hindu cosmology. There are five towers at the center of the temple. They symbolize the five mountain peaks. The temple is surrounded by a moat and three galleries. A moat is deep, broad depression in the ground that is usually filled with water and surrounds a structure. The ground of the temple symbolizes the world and the wall stands for the mountains at the edge of the world. The surroundings of the temple stand for the shore and the oceans.

Building material

The Angkor Wat temple and other buildings in Cambodia were originally built from wood. The wood temples were built in the same way as the later simple brick temples. Bricks were manufactured in Cambodia from early times. However, very little variety of stones was available at that time. Laterite and sandstone became the primary building material during the 13th century. The Angkor Wat temple was built using sandstone and laterite. As the sandstone was not available in the immediate area, it had been carried far away from Phnom Kulen. The sandstone was transported to the construction site through a river. A vast army of slaves, builders, and craftsmen were used to carry the sandstone and to transport it to the site. There the architects and crafts men worked on the stones and carved them to create the beautiful temple.

Angkor Wat temple complex

Satellite image of the Great Barrier Reef

Great Barrier Reef

The Great Barrier Reef is one of the natural wonders of the world. It is the world's largest coral reef ecosystem. It extends along the northeast coast of Queensland, Australia for about 2000 km.

The Great Barrier Reef is the best-known marine protected area in the world. It covers an area of approximately 344210 sq km. and is scattered with a number of beautiful islands and around 3000 coral reefs. The reefs range in size from 340,224 sq km to over 100 sq km in area.

Coral

Corals form reefs and cays. Corals grow in shallow, warm water. They need sufficient light, and highly saline water to grow. A coral consists of individual coral polyps. Polyps are tiny creatures, which group together and form colonies. Each polyp lives inside a hard shell. This shell is generally known as the coral.

Coral

Marine life

The Great Barrier Reef has a great diversity of marine life. It is one of the most valued ecosystems in the world. The reef is home to many endangered and endemic species. It has around 1500 species of fish, a large number of whales and dolphins, 4000 types of molluscs and many varieties of seaweeds, sea snakes, sea turtles and dugongs. Other creatures present in large numbers include anemones, marine worms, crustaceans (prawns, crabs etc.) and echinoderms (starfish, sea urchins etc.).

Sea turtles are abundant in the Great Barrier Reef

Barrier reefs

Barrier reefs are reefs formed parallel to the coastline. They are separated from the shore by a wide, deep lagoon. Barrier reefs are so called because they provide a barrier between the ocean and the shore.

Importance of coral reef

Coral reefs are important in many ways. They provide shelter as well as protection to many species of marine animals. These reefs also protect coasts from strong currents and waves by slowing down the water before it gets to the shore.

Climate

The Great Barrier Reef varies in climatic conditions. It is located between the continental island of Australia and the open ocean of the south Pacific. The climate is strongly influenced by both the neighboring land mass and oceanic effects. The climate varies from north to south. The south has a cooler climate with subtropical to temperate conditions. The north has tropical humid conditions with a wet season in January. The rainfall in this region is seasonal and varies geographically.

World Heritage Site

The Great Barrier Reef was inscribed as a world heritage site in 1981 because of its unique size and variety of plants and animals. It is one of the richest natural areas on Earth. The reef now lies within the Great Barrier Reef marine park, which is the largest marine park in the world. This park has an area of about 345,600 sq km. The Great Barrier Reef represents the ongoing ecological and biological processes of the Earth.

Threats

The Great Barrier Reef faces significant threats global warming, pollution and declining due to water quality. Rising ocean temperatures have led to frequent coral bleaching. Climate change has also affected the population of sea turtles found in the area. Water pollution has led to a decrease in the growth of corals. The coral reef also faces major threat from starfish. Starfish are natural predators of corals.

A view of the vast expanse of the Grand Canyon

Grand Canyon

The Grand Canyon is one of the natural wonders of the world. It is a deep, wide gorge carved by the Colorado River in northern Arizona, USA. It is one of the most beautiful canyons of the world.

The Grand Canyon lies in the southwestern portion of the Colorado plateau. The mighty Colorado River has cut through the rocks of the Colorado plateau for about 6 million years forming the canyon. The canyon is 43.2 km long, 6.4 to 28.8 km wide, and is more than a mile deep at places.

Colorado plateau

The Colorado plateau is a large beautiful plateau in southwestern United States. It is characterized by horizontal, layered rocks, lava flows, deep canyons, barren, and dry lands. The climate is dry and arid and the area is sparsely vegetated. The plateau covers an area of around 332,850 sq km and has an average elevation of 1500 m. It includes areas drained by the Colorado River and its territories. The Grand Canyon section of the plateau is the highest section of the Colorado plateau.

The two rims

The North Rim of the Grand Canyon is approximately 2500 m. It is around 366 m higher than the South Rim. The average width between the two rims is around 16 km. The North Rim is remote. It also has a comparatively cool weather and experiences heavy snowfall in winters.
The South Rim is the busiest and the most developed part. It has a pleasant climate for most part of the year, although winters in this rim are extreme like the North Rim.

García Lopez de Cardenas

Garcia Lopez de Cardenas was a Spanish explorer. He was the first European to explore the Grand Canyon in 1540.

Grand Canyon National park

The Grand Canyon National Park covers the deepest and the most beautiful sections of the Canyon. It covers an area of 4864 sq km. The park is a world heritage site and was established as a national monument in 1908 and as a national park in 1919. The natural beauty of the park attracts about 3 million visitors yearly. The headquarters of the park are located at the Grand Canyon Village.

Eroded rocks of the canyon

Rock layers

The rocks and the walls of the Grand Canyon are a living timeline of the Earth's history over the past 6 million years. The rocks at the bottom of the canyon are 2.5 billion years old. These rocks are known as Vishnu Schist to geologists.
A 540 million years old layer of limestone overlies the granite and schist layer. On top of these two layers is a layer of limestone, freshwater shale, and cemented sandstones. This forms a large part of the canyon's walls. Most of the rock layers added over the past thousand years and sheets of lava deposits of the recent past have been removed by erosion.

Flora and fauna

The Grand Canyon has varied flora and fauna. The bottom of the canyon has mostly drought-resistant trees such as agave and varieties of cactus as the region receives scanty rainfall and remains dry for most part of the year. The rims however, have a wide variety of plants. The forests of the south rim are abundant with species of pine, mahogany and oak. The Grand Canyon is also home to a large number of animals such as squirrels, coyotes, foxes, deer, badgers, bobcats, rabbits, chipmunks, and kangaroo rats.

Archeological findings

Human artifacts that are thousands of years old have been found on the Grand Canyon. Most of the remains belong to the Paleo-Indian, Archaic, Basketmaker, Ancestral Puebloan, Cohonina, Cerbat, Pai, Zuni, Hopi, Navajo, and Euro-American culture groups. One of the most fascinating finds at the Grand Canyon are the split-twig figurines. These are small animal figurines made using a single twig split in the middle. They are around 2000 to 4000 years old.

Colorado River

The Colorado River flows from the Rocky mountains to the Gulf of California in the US. It is 2320 km long. It is the main force behind the creation of the beautiful Grand Canyon. The river is 853 m above the sea level at the North Rim and 762 m above sea level at the South Rim of the Grand Canyon.

Himalayas

The Himalayas are a mountain range on the border of India and Tibet. They are also known as Himyan, Himvat, Himachal and Himadri. The range stretches across six nations: Bhutan, China, India, Nepal, Pakistan, and Afghanistan.

The Himalayan mountain range is one of the youngest mountain ranges on Earth. It consists of some of the highest peaks of the world. More than 30 peaks of the Himalayas have a height of 7620 m or more. The world's highest mountain Mount Everest lies in the Himalayas.

Formation

The Himalayas were formed as a result of plate tectonics. Millions of years ago, all the continents were a single continent called Pangaea. About 200 million years ago, when Pangaea broke apart, the Indian sub-continent began to forge northward. When two large landmasses, India and Eurasia driven by plate movement collided, neither of the plates could be subducted under the other. This happened because both plates had almost the same rock density. This collision thrust the plates skywards and formed the jagged Himalayan peaks.

Classification

The Himalayas have been grouped into four parallel, longitudinal mountain belts, from south to north. They are the Sub-Himalayas or the Shivaliks, the Lesser Himalayas or the Himachal, the Great Himalayas or Himadri, and the Trans-Himalayas or the Tibetan Himalayas. They have also been classified on the basis of international political boundaries as the Indian Himalayas, Nepalese Himalayas, and the Tibetan Himalayas.

The Himalayan mountain range

Mount Everest

Mount Everest, the highest mountain in the world, is located in the Himalayan range on the frontier of Tibet and Nepal. It is 8848 m high. It is a young mountain, formed of limestone rock. It is believed that the height of the Mount Everest increases by about 0.5 cm every year. The Everest got its name from a British military engineer, Sir George Everest, who was the director of the Great Trigonometrical Survey of India between 1830 and 1843. Sir Edmund Hillary of New Zealand and Tensing Norgay of Nepal became the first men to reach the top of Everest on 29 May 1953.

Sub-Himalayas

The Sub-Himalayas are the lowest range in the Himalayan system. This range forms the southernmost belt of the Himalayan range. It rises steeply from the northern plains of India and Pakistan. It runs parallel to the main ranges of the Himalayas towards the north. The Sub-Himalayan range is also known as Shivalik. The name "Shivalik" is a Sanskrit word that means belonging to the Hindu god, Lord Shiva.

Lesser Himalayas

The Lesser Himalayas form the middle section of the Himalayan mountain chain. The range extends southeast from Pakistan and passes through the large parts of the Indian states of Jammu and Kashmir, Himachal Pradesh, and Western Uttar Pradesh. It extends to Nepal and the North-Eastern Himalayas. It is also known as Himachal.

Great Himalayas

Great Himalayas are the northernmost, longest and the most continuous belt in the Himalayan system. They lie well above the snow line with an average elevation of about 6100 m. They rise to their maximum height in Nepal. They contain nine of the fourteen highest peaks in the world, all above 8000 m above sea level. The highest mountain, Mount Everest also lies there. Great Himalayas are also called Himadri.

Indian Himalayas

The Indian Himalayas are a part of the Himalayan mountain range that runs through the entire northern region of India. The range covers a vast area along the northern frontiers of the country. It spans across five Indian States—Jammu and Kashmir, Himachal Pradesh, Uttar Pradesh, Sikkim, and Arunachal Pradesh. The Indian Himalayas can be divided into many ranges: Kashmir, Ladakh, Zanskar, Lahaul and Spiti, Chamba, Kinnaur, Kumaon, Garhwal, Sikkim, and Arunachal.

Trans-Himalayan range (Tibetan Himalayas)

The Trans-Himalayan range is a region that covers the Tibetan plateau. The region covers an area of about 1000 km. The southern part of Tibet, the highest plateau in the world, falls within the Himalayan region. Mt Everest (8848 m), Namcha Barwa (7756 m) and Gurla Mandhata (7728 m) define the southern border of Tibet.

Nepalese Himalayas

The Himalayan range in Nepal has nine of the world's fourteen highest peaks. The range covers three-fourths of the land of Nepal. The world's highest mountain peak, Mt Everest, also lies in Nepal. Lhotse, Nuptse, Annapurna, Dhaulagiri, Manaslu are examples of the other high peaks.

Angel Falls

The Angel Falls (Salto Angel) is one of the natural wonders of the world. Located in southeastern Venezuela, South America, Angel Falls is the highest free-falling waterfall in the world.

The fall drops from a height of 979 m from the mesa of Auyán Tepuy (Devil's Mountain) in the Guiana Highlands. The Auyán Tepui is a flat-topped mountain. It has an uninterrupted drop of 800 m and is 150 m wide at its base. The falls drains all its water into the River Churun, which flows at its base. Angel Falls was discovered in 1935 by an American aviator and adventurer James C. Angel.

Guiana highlands

The Guiana highlands is a mountainous region. It lies south of the Orinoco River, in northern South America. The highland is also known as Guiana Shield or Guiana Massif. It extends from Venezuela into Guyana and northern Brazil. The highlands are a source of some of the most spectacular waterfalls in the world such as Angel Falls, Kaieteur Falls, and Kuquenan Falls.

Jimmy Crawford Angel (1899-1956)

Angel Falls is named after James "Jimmy" Crawford Angel, who made it known to the Western world. Jimmy Angel was an American aviator and adventurer. He first saw the Angel Falls in 1933, when he was searching for a valuable ore bed. Jimmy returned there in 1936 with his wife and gardener.

Churun and Caroni Rivers

The Churun River is located in the Canaima National Park. The river flows from the world's highest waterfalls, Angel Falls. The Caroni River lies in the southeastern Venezuela. It is 676 km long and the Angel Falls lie on a headstream of the river. It flows northward across the Guiana Highlands. The river covers most of the southeastern region. It drops into the Orinoco River at San Felix, in the Ciudad Guiana area.

Canaima Lagoon

Canaima National Park

The Canaima National Park is the main gateway to the Angel Falls. The park is spread over around 296,44.8 sq km, along the border between Guyana and Brazil. Almost 65 per cent of the park is covered by table-like mountains known as tepui. The park was established on 12 June 1962. It was inscribed as a world heritage site in 1994. Canaima National Park includes the uplands of Gran and protects a section of the Guyana Shield. It is covered with thick forests, savannahs and has many spectacular waterfalls. It is home to many species of birds, lizards, snakes, and mammals. Most of Guiana's hydraulic resources lie within the park, such as Caroni River, which feeds the Raul Leoni dam.

Ernesto de Santa Cruz

Ernesto de Santa Cruz was the first discoverer of the Angel Falls. He found the Angel Falls in 1910 but did not publicise his discovery. They were not known to the outside world till the American aviator, James Crawford Angel, flew over them on 16 November 1933.

Angel Falls

Niagara Falls

The Niagara Falls is a group of the three falls located on the Niagara River on the border of United States and Canada. The three falls that make up the great falls are the Horseshoe or Canadian Falls, American Falls, and Bridal Veil Falls. The Niagara Falls is the most famous and most visited waterfall in the world.

The Niagara Falls was probably formed about 12,000 years ago. A great ice sheet melted from the region caused Lake Erie to flow. The river cut through a ridge (escarpment) that extends from southern Ontario to Rochester, New York. The process continued over the centuries and formed the Niagara Falls. The Niagara Falls was first discovered by Louis Hennepin, a Roman Catholic priest, in 1678.

Niagara's Horseshoe falls

Horseshoe or Canadian Falls

The Horseshoe Falls is one of the three falls at the Niagara Falls. It is located mostly on the Canadian side of the border with the United States. It is located between Table Rock House in Ontario and Terrapin Point on Goat Island in New York. It is about 51 m high and 792 m wide at its widest point. In 1721, it was first described as "horseshoe-shaped". So, it is also called Horseshoe Falls.

Goat Island and Luna Islands

Goat Island is a small island in New York located in the middle of the Niagara River, between the Bridal Veil and Canadian Falls. The island lies at the southwestern tip of Niagara County. Luna Island is located to the south of American Falls. It is separated from Goat Island by the Bridal Veil Falls.

American Falls

The American Falls is one of the three Niagara Falls. It is slightly higher than its Canadian counterpart. It is about 54 m high and 395 m wide. About 75,000 gallons of water flow over the American Falls each second. This amounts to 10 per cent of Niagara's total water flow. The falls is visible from a steep angle on the American side. One can view the falls from the bank of the river and on the Goat Island. The ledge of the American Falls is shaped in a modified "W" form. This shape has been caused by numerous rockfalls over the past 150 years.

Bridal Veil falls

The Bridal Veil Falls is the smallest of the three Niagara waterfalls. It is located between Luna Island and Goat Island that separates it from the American and Horseshoe Falls. The Bridal Veil Falls faces to the northwest. Its crest is 17 m wide.

Niagara River

The Niagara River is a short river. It is only about 56 km long. It begins at the Eastern end of Lake Erie at Buffalo, New York. It is often called a "Strait" that means a narrow channel of water that connects two larger bodies of water, Lake Erie and Lake Ontario. The spectacular Niagara Falls is located about midway down the river. The river has four distinct sections:

1. The Upper Niagara River
2. The Cascades and the Falls
3. The American Goat Island Channel
4. The Lower Niagara River

Though the river is quite a small one, no man has been able to traverse the length of the river. Ships cannot sail the full length of the river because of falls and rapids. The water level and speed of the water is controlled by wind. The southwest winds over Lake Erie increase the speed and the water level. The east winds across Lake Erie reduce the water speed and water level.

Hoover Dam

The Hoover dam is one of the architectural wonders of the world. It is one of the highest concrete dams in the world. The dam is in the Black Canyon on the Colorado River, southeast of Las Vegas, Nevada.

The Hoover dam is the highest and the third largest concrete dam in the United States. It was built as a part of the Boulder Canyon Project. The other parts of the project were a hydroelectric power plant and a reservoir. The dam is 379 m long with a height of 220 m from the foundation rock. It generates more than 4 billion kilowatt-hours of power every year.

Colorado river and its basin

The Colorado River flows from the snow-capped Rocky mountains and zigzags its way to the Gulf of California. It travels for almost 2240 km before it reaches the Gulf. The river along with its tributaries – the Green, the Gunnison, the San Juan, the Virgin, the Little Colorado, and the Gila rivers – is collectively called the Colorado River Basin. The states of Arizona, California, Colorado, Nevada, New Mexico, Utah, and Wyoming are called the Colorado River Basin States.

Hydroelectric power plant

The power plant located at the base of the Hoover dam generates low-cost hydroelectric power for use in the states of Nevada, Arizona, and California. The plant is a U-shaped structure and has some of the largest generators and turbines. It is one of the largest hydroelectric power plants in the United States. It is operated and maintained by the Bureau of Reclamation, U.S. Department of Interior.

Lake Mead–the Hoover Dam reservoir

The dam

The Hoover dam is one of the largest masonry structures in the world. It was built to control the floods of the Colorado River, generate hydroelectricity and supply domestic and irrigation water to a large area of the Pacific southwest. The construction of the dam began on 20 April 1931. It took five years to complete the concrete placement. The last concrete was placed on 29 May 1935, and the other features of the dam was completed by 1936. The concrete used was made of sand, crushed rock, water and Portland cement. A total of 21,000 men were employed for the construction of the great dam.

Benefits of the dam

Hoover Dam provides many benefits:

- It controls the floods in the Colorado River.
- It provides water for irrigation to the fertile but arid agricultural regions of California and Arizona.
- It satisfies the power requirements of millions of people in adjacent areas through its hydroelectric power plant.

Diverted route

During the course of the construction of the dam, the Colorado River had to be diverted from its route. Four tunnels were built through the walls of the Black canyon and the river flowed through them for almost five years.

Six Companies Inc.

The Hoover dam was built by a construction company called Six Companies Inc. The company actually was a group of six major companies that included Morrison-Knudsen Co., Utah Construction Co., J. F. Shea Co., Pacific Bridge Co., MacDonald & Kahn Ltd. and a joint venture of W. A. Bechtel Co., Henry J. Kaiser, and Warren Brothers. The collaboration happened as there was no single construction company that could invest $5 million needed to secure the performance bond.

Naming the dam

The Hoover Dam was known by various names till President Harry S. Truman signed a resolution on 30 April 1947 naming the dam after the 31st U.S President, Mr. Herbert Hoover. President Truman recognized the efforts made by Hoover and the part he played in the entire construction of the dam during his presidential tenure. The dam was officially named Hoover dam for the first time in 1931. In 1932, Hoover lost the Presidential elections and Franklin Roosevelt came into power. Then, the dam was renamed Boulder Dam.

Lake Mead

Lake Mead is the reservoir of the Hoover dam. It is one of the largest man-made lakes. The lake extends 184 km upstream, and is 1.6-16 km wide. It was named after Elwood Mead, who was the commissioner of the U.S. Bureau of Reclamation during the planning and construction of the Boulder Canyon Project.

Galapagos Islands

Galapagos Islands are one of the most fascinating places on Earth. They are an archipelago in the Pacific Ocean. They are located about 960 km west of Ecuador, in northwestern South America. The Galapagos Islands group has 13 major islands and 6 smaller ones. The group is also called the Archipelago de Colon.

The Galapagos Islands cover a total land area of 7915.52 sq km scattered over 58810.88 sq km of the ocean. Human population is scarce. There are only around 6000 people living on the islands. The Galapagos Islands are known for the wide variety of indigenous fauna.

Discovery

Fray Tomas de Berlanga, the bishop of Panama was the first person to visit the islands in 1535. He discovered the islands accidentally when he was sailing to Peru to settle a dispute between Francisco Pizarro and his lieutenants after the conquest of the Incas. His ship stalled when the winds died and strong currents carried him out to the Galapagos. Berlanga, later in his writings described the harsh, desert-like condition of the islands. He also wrote about the large tortoises that Galapagos are known for, the marine iguanas, the sea lions and the many types of birds.

Darwin's observations

Charles Darwin was the first to make a scientific study of the Galapagos Islands in 1835. He studied many different species of birds, tortoises and iguanas that inhabited the islands and made an astonishing observation. He observed that the giant tortoises found on all the islands differed from each other. He also found that many of the birds, especially the land birds, were endemic species found nowhere else on Earth. Darwin maintained throughout his life that the Galapagos Islands were the source of all his ideas and research. Because of Darwin's observation, the Galapagos are today most closely associated with Darwin.

Galapagos Islands

Isabela Island

Isabela Island is the largest island of the archipelago. It covers an area of 4536.32 sq km. It is shaped like a sea horse and is lined with a chain of active volcanoes. Geologically, the island is one of the most volcanically active places on earth. Wolf volcano, at a height of 1700 m, is the highest peak on the island. Isabela Island is also known for its rich flora and fauna. It is home to the highest number of Galapagos tortoises. Some of the tortoises found on the island spend most of their time wallowing in the mud at the volcano craters. This characteristic of Galapagos tortoises has not been noticed in any other tortoise species.

Galapagos tortoises

Ferdinanda Island

Ferdinanda island is located on the west side of Isabela islands. It is one of the most volcanically active islands. It covers an area of 634 sq km. It is the third largest and the youngest of all the Galapagos Islands. It is home to a large colony of Marine Iguanas, Galapagos Penguins and Flightless Cormorants. However, no human population is found on the Island.

Santa Cruz Island

Santa Cruz is the central island of the Galapagos Island. It covers an area of 993.28 sq km. It is the most highly populated Galapagos Island. It also receives the highest number of visitors. The Galapagos National Park Service and the Charles Darwin research centre are located on the Island. Santa Cruz Island is also known as "Chaves" and its official Ecuadorian name is "Isla Santa Cruz."

World Heritage Site

The Galapagos Islands have been declared a World Heritage Site by UNESCO. The islands are owned by Ecuador and are maintained as part of the nation's national park system.

Galapagos seals

Eiffel Tower

The Eiffel tower is a huge iron tower on the Champ de Mars in Paris. The tower was built for the 1889 World's Fair to be held as a celebration for the French revolution centenary.

The Eiffel Tower is probably Europe's best-known landmark and Paris's most famous symbol. It is 300 m high. The tower has a television antenna on top that gives it a total elevation of 322 m. The height of the base of the tower is 5 m. The Tower was inaugurated on 31 March 1889 by the Prince of Wales, later king Edward VII of England.

Construction

The 300 m tall Eiffel Tower was the tallest man-made structure in the world until the completion of the Chrysler Building in New York City in 1930. The construction of the tower began on 23 January 1887 and took a little more than two years to be completed. The tower has 1665 steps and transparent lifts that go up to the 2nd floor. The tower was constructed using 18,038 pieces of puddled iron (a pure form of structural iron). Around 300 workers were employed to join the iron. The total weight of the structure is 10,100 metric tonnes. The cost of construction of the tower came to almost $1.5 million.

Colour

The Eiffel tower is painted with several layers of paint to protect the iron from oxidation. On an average the tower is painted once every seven years. Over the years, the tower has been painted in different shades of brown ranging from red-brown to bronze. The most recent repainting operation began in 2001 and lasted for two years. It was the 18th coat of paint applied on the tower.

Structure

The lower section of the tower has four arched legs that extend upwards and unite in a single tapered tower. The tower has three platforms and each platform has an observation deck. The uppermost observation deck is at a height of 275 m. The tower has a meteorological station, a television transmission antenna and a radio station. It has two restaurants, one on the first floor and the other on the second floor. The tower also has a suite of rooms near the top. These rooms were used by Eiffel.

Architects

The Eiffel Tower was designed and built by Gustave Eiffel. Maurice Koechlin, Emile Nougier and Stephen Sauvestre were the co-architects of the tower.

Alexandre Gustave Eiffel (1832-1923)

Alexandre Gustave Eiffel was born in Dijon, France in 1832. He was an engineer and architect. Eiffel established his career as an engineer-contractor. Eiffel was a master of wrought-iron lattices, which led to his project for the Eiffel Tower. Eiffel is also well known for designing the armature for the Statue of Liberty, in New York, USA. Eiffel died in Paris in 1923.

Seventy two names

The tower has names of seventy-two French scientists, engineers and some other notable people, engraved on it. The names were engraved by Gustave Eiffel in recognition of their contributions to the construction of the tower.

The antenna

The Eiffel tower has an antennae at its top. In 1909, the tower was saved from being torn down because of the presence of the antenna that was used for telegraphy at that time.

Eiffel Tower lit up at night

Lighting the tower

From gas to electricity, the tower has been illuminated using various methods over the years. The first lighting system at the Eiffel tower was installed for the Universal Exposition of 1900. In 1925, André Citroën lit up the tower with his coloured lighting A.D. campaign. The present lighting system has been in place since 1985. It has 352 sodium yellow-orange tint lamps, placed on the inside of the tower. These lamps beautifully light up the intricate structure of the tower. The tower also has 2 light beams that can be seen from about 8 km away.

Eiffel Tower

Statue of Liberty

Liberty Enlightening the World or the Statue of Liberty stands at the Liberty Island, New York. It was a gift from France to the United States in 1886, on its first centennial of independence. The statue is also known as Lady Liberty.

The Statue of Liberty symbolises liberty from oppression and tyranny. It is the statue of a woman in a robe, holding a torch burning with the light of freedom. She is adorned with a diadem with seven-spikes and holds a stone tablet in her left hand. The tablet bears the words "JULY IV MDCCLXXVI" (4 July 1776), the date of American independence. Broken chains lie at Lady Liberty's feet symbolising freedom from the reign of terror and cruelty.

Designers

Lady Liberty was designed by a French sculptor, Frédéric-Auguste Bartholdi. In 1871, Bartholdi chose Liberty Island as the site of the monument during his trip to the United States. The internal structure of the statue was designed by Gustave Eiffel, the designer of the famous Eiffel Tower.
Eiffel made the internal framework of steel and covered it with copper sheets.

The statue

The Statue of Liberty is one of the largest statues in the world. The statue stands on a pedestal. The height of the statue from the ground to the tip of the torch is 93.5 m. The height of just the statue is 46 m. The statue weighs about 226 tonnes. The torch of the statue has 16 powerful lamps arranged around the rim. The lamps glow brightly at night.

Funds

The construction of the statue began in 1875 in Paris. The funds required for the construction of the statue were raised from public donations and by hosting various forms of popular public shows. A charitable lottery was also used to raise the funds required. The pedestal of the statue was built in America. Its construction started in 1884 and was completed in 1886. The United States too raised the required money for the construction of the pedestal in a similar way by organising public shows and auctions.

Visit to the statue

The Statue of Liberty can be visited by ferry from the Manhattan Island. Visitors can reach the pedestal by climbing 189 stairs. The observation area in the crown has a platform with 25 windows. The platform can hold around 20 people at a time. Visitors are not allowed to visit the torch area.

The pedestal

The pedestal is the base on which the statue stands. It is a mass of concrete made with steel beams covered with granite. The pedestal starts from the walls of a star-shaped fort. The fort was built in 1806 for the defence of New York from naval attacks. The total height of the pedestal and the fort is 47 m. The pedestal was designed by an architect, Richard Morris Hunt of the United States.

The statue

Dedication

The people of France presented the statue to the people of United States to commemorate the centennial of US independence. The statue was disassembled into 214 pieces and packed in wooden crates and shipped to the United States. It was assembled there and was placed on the pedestal, where it stands now. The statue was officially dedicated by President Grover Cleveland in New York City on 28 October 1886.

The pedestal

Golden Gate Bridge

The Golden Gate Bridge is one of the modern wonders of the world. The bridge spans the Golden Gate strait. It stretches from northern California to the peninsula of San Francisco and connects the city of San Francisco to Marin County, California, United States.

The Golden Gate Bridge is a principal landmark of San Francisco and California. It is a about 2730 m long suspension bridge with the longest single span of 1280 m. It is one of the longest bridges in the United States.

Golden Gate strait

The Golden Gate strait is a channel at the entrance to the San Francisco Bay that separates the bay from the Pacific Ocean. It is 7.8 km long, and more than a kilometre wide. The strait was named Golden Gate in 1846 by an American explorer John Charles Frémont.

Construction

The planning of the construction of the Golden Gate Bridge started in 1928. However, its actual construction started in January, 1933. The bridge was completed after four and a half years in May, 1937. The grand opening of the Golden Gate Bridge was celebrated by over 20,000 people by walking the length of the bridge.

Architects

Joseph Strauss was the chief architect and engineer who initiated and headed the construction of the Golden Gate Bridge. The construction of the bridge at that location was a difficult task because of extreme weather conditions. Another significant challenge was that the bridge would stand less than 13 km from the epicenter of the most disastrous earthquake in history. At that point only Strauss was willing to take up the challenge of constructing the bridge. Two other engineers, who contributed immensely to the construction were Charles Alton Ellis and famed bridge designer, Leon Moisseiff.

Golden Gate Bridge overlooking the San Francisco harbour

A view of one of the Golden Gate Bridge towers

The bridge

The bridge is supported by two tall towers on both the ends. The towers are the first structures that are seen from the ships approaching San Francisco. They hold up two steel cables that help the bridge hang. The distance between the towers is the longest span and measures about 1280 m. The floor of the bridge is 67 m above water and is 27 m wide. The bridge has six reversible lanes that help the traffic flow during the commuting hours.

Colour

The colour of the Golden Gate Bridge is orange vermillion which is also known as International orange. The colour was suggested by Irving Morrow, an architect as the colour blended with the natural surrounding of the bridge. The colour also enhances the bridge's visibility in fog.

Plaques

The Golden Gate Bridge has two plaques. One of them acknowledges the names of the officers, past officers, directors, past directors, engineering staff, and contractors involved in the construction of the Golden Gate Bridge. The other is a memorial plaque at the southern entrance. It also acknowledges the eleven men killed during the construction of the bridge.

Fort Point

Fort Point, at the south end of the bridge, was built out of brick in 1853–1861. It was designated a National Historic Monument on 16 October 1970. The historic fort was used as a base of operations for building the Golden Gate Bridge. The Fort Point Lighthouse was the second lighthouse built in California.

Suez Canal

Suez Canal

The Suez Canal in Egypt is an artificial waterway. The canal connects the Mediterranean Sea to the Red Sea. It provides a shortcut route between the European and American ports and the ports in southern Asia, eastern Africa, and Oceania.

The Suez Canal is one of the most important waterways in the world. It is often called the "Crossroads of Europe, Africa, and Asia" as it is used to transport goods to and from all three continents. The construction of the canal considerably reduced the distance between the continents. After the canal was completed in 1869, the distance between India and the United Kingdom was shortened by almost 9600 km.

Physical features

The Suez Canal is 161.6 km long. Over the years, the canal has been widened to handle the growing traffic. At the time of its construction the canal was 8 m deep but now it is 19 m deep. The minimum bottom and surface width of the canal too has increased. Initially it was 22 m wide at the bottom and 70 m wide at the surface. Now the bottom is 92 m wide and surface width is 226 m.
The canal can accommodate ships as large as 150,000 dead weight tonnes fully loaded. The canal utilises three bodies of water—Lake Manzilah, Lake Timsāh, and the Bitter Lakes. The transit time is only 15 hours as it connects two points at sea level without any high ground. The traffic on most of the canal is limited to a single lane but two lane bypasses are also located in certain places.

History

The idea of the construction of a canal to link the Mediterranean and the Red Sea dates back to ancient times. Canals were built to connect the two water bodies hundreds of years before the birth of Christ. Around 1800 A.D., one of Napoleon's engineers revived the idea of a shorter trade route to India through a canal on the Suez. The construction of the present Suez Canal was proposed by French diplomat and engineer, Vicomte Ferdinand Marie de Lesseps. Ferdinand Marie de Lesseps obtained permission for the project from the Ruler of Egypt, Said Pasha in 1854. In 1855, an international technical commission planned the route of the canal and the Suez Canal Company was formed to dig and operate the canal in 1858.

The Suez Canal during it's construction

Construction

The construction of the canal began in 1859, and was completed in 1869. The canal was inaugurated during the ruling of El Khedive Ismael on 17 November 1869 in an elaborate ceremony. During the construction of the canal, a total of 73.99 million cubic metres of earth had to be moved. The cost of the construction of the canal was about $65 million. Most of it was funded by the French.

A satellite view of the Suez Canal

Sydney Opera House

The Sydney Opera House is one of the architectural wonders of the world. The opera house is located in Sydney, New South Wales, Australia. It is situated on Bennelong Point, which reaches out into Sydney Harbour's Port Jackson. The opera house was designed by Danish architect Jorn Utzon.

The opera house is a complex of halls and theatres, which are linked together. The house presents theatre, musicals, opera, contemporary dance, ballet, and every form of music from symphony concerts to jazz as well as exhibitions and films. It is also used for other functions such as parties, conferences and weddings. The house operates 24 hours a day, every day of the year except Christmas Day and Good Friday.

Conception

The idea of constructing the Sydney Opera House arose after World War II. In 1954, the government of South Wales decided to build a new opera house. The Bennelong Point was finalised as a site for the opera house. Architects from all over the world were invited to submit their designs for a complex including two main halls, a restaurant and public meeting rooms. The competition was announced and in December, 1956, a total of 234 architects from nine different countries submitted their designs. The results were announced in January 1957 and a Danish architect, John Utzon won the competition.

Construction

The formal construction of the opera house began in March, 1959. The project was divided into three stages. The first stage consisted of building the upper podium that was constructed between 1959-1963. The second stage involved building the outer shells and the third stage involved the interior design and construction. The third stage took four years to complete and was completed between 1967-1973.

Funds

The funds for the construction of the Sydney Opera House were largely provided by a lottery system. Before the construction started, many public fund-raising campaigns were organised to collect money. The campaigns failed to produce sufficient funding and an opera lottery house was created in 1958. The lottery continued till the completion of the opera house.

Inauguration

The Sydney Opera House took 17 years to complete. It was inaugurated by Queen Elizabeth II, on 20 October 1973. The opening ceremony of the opera house was attended by millions of people. The programme was televised and included a performance of Beethoven's symphony number 9 along with a fireworks show.

Problems

Jorn Utzon faced many technical problems during the construction of the opera house. His design required advanced technology, which was not available at that point of time. So, the construction was delayed by several years. During this period, Utzon was pressurised by the government and the press to continue the project and ignore his problems. John Utzon, however, refused to do so, and he resigned and returned to Denmark in 1965. After his resignation, the construction of the opera house was handed over to a group of Australian architects. The opera house was finally completed in 1973. The total cost incurred amounted to almost 15 times the estimated budget.

Sydney Opera House

Petronas Towers

The Petronas Towers in Kuala Lumpur, Malaysia are the second tallest buildings of the world. The towers are also known as the Petronas twin towers. Petronas is short for *Petroliam Nasional Bhd*, Malaysia's national petroleum corporation. The twin towers were built to house the headquarters of Petronas. The towers have shopping and entertainment facilities, a petroleum museum, a symphony hall, a mosque, and a multimedia conference centre.

The towers are set in the heart of the city. Both the towers have 88 stories that rise to a height of 378 m. The total height of the towers is 452 m and they cover an area of 427,353 sq. m. The towers are joined by a flexible skybridge on the 41st and 42nd floor. The towers were considered the tallest buildings in the world by the Council on Tall Buildings and Urban Habitat until the completion of Taipei 101.

Architect and architecture

The Petronas towers were designed by Pelli Clarke Pelli Architects (formerly known as Cesar Pelli and Associates). The towers have a simple geometric form that is common in Muslim architecture. The exterior of the towers has two interlocking squares that form an eight-pointed star. Eight semi-circles are placed upon the eight-pointed stars to soften the inner angles. The circular pattern of the buildings rise and gradually taper at the upper levels. The exterior of the towers is organised in horizontal ribbons of vision glass and stainless steel which glint and shimmer in the sun. The interior of the towers shows the beauty and tradition of Malaysian arts and handicrafts.

The Petronas Twin Towers

Pinnacles

The peaks or top of the Petronas towers are made of structural steel. The pinnacles of the towers are 73.5 m tall. One pinnacle was fabricated in Japan and the other was made in Korea. Each pinnacle has a spire, mast ball and ring ball.

The sky bridge of the Petronas Twin Towers

Sky bridge

The sky bridge on the 41st and 42nd floors that connects the two towers was constructed to ease travel between the towers. It is a double-decked sky bridge and it can also function as an escape route in an emergency. The bridge is supported by a three-hinged arch, which consists of giant round bearings at the base. It has a pair of cylindrical legs that is 51 m long. The legs are locked to a box girder below the centre of the bridge.

Elevator system

The Petronas towers are equipped with 29 double-decker, high-speed passenger lifts. There are four executive lifts and six heavy-duty service lifts in each tower. The elevators are designed to serve every floor of the tower. The lifts can transport passengers from the basement car parking to the top of the towers.

Foundation and inauguration

The construction of the Petronas towers was completed in many phases. The plan for constructing the towers began in January 1992. The foundation work of the towers started in March 1992. The towers were inaugurated by Dato Seri Dr. Mahathir bin Mohamad, the 4th Prime Minister of Malaysia on 31 August 1999.

Kansai International Airport

The Kansai International Airport is the world's first ocean airport. It is located on an artificial island in the Osaka Bay, in Japan. The airport is considered one of the modern engineering wonders of the world.

The Kansai airport was constructed to handle the city's growing international traffic. It is connected to the mainland by a highway bridge. The construction of the airport also helped protect the local environment and control noise pollution. It is Japan's first airport to provide 24 hour services.

Construction

The Kansai International Airport was built on an artificial island. The construction of the island began in 1987. The first step involved the building of a sea wall using rocks and concrete. The wall was completed in 1989. After the completion of the wall, the area within the wall was filled with earth to create the artificial island. Almost 10,000 workers were employed to do this. Once the island was built, a 2.88 km long bridge was built to connect it to the mainland in 1990. The construction of the airport terminal began in 1991 and the airport was inaugurated on 4 September 1994.

Satellite view of the Kansai International Airport

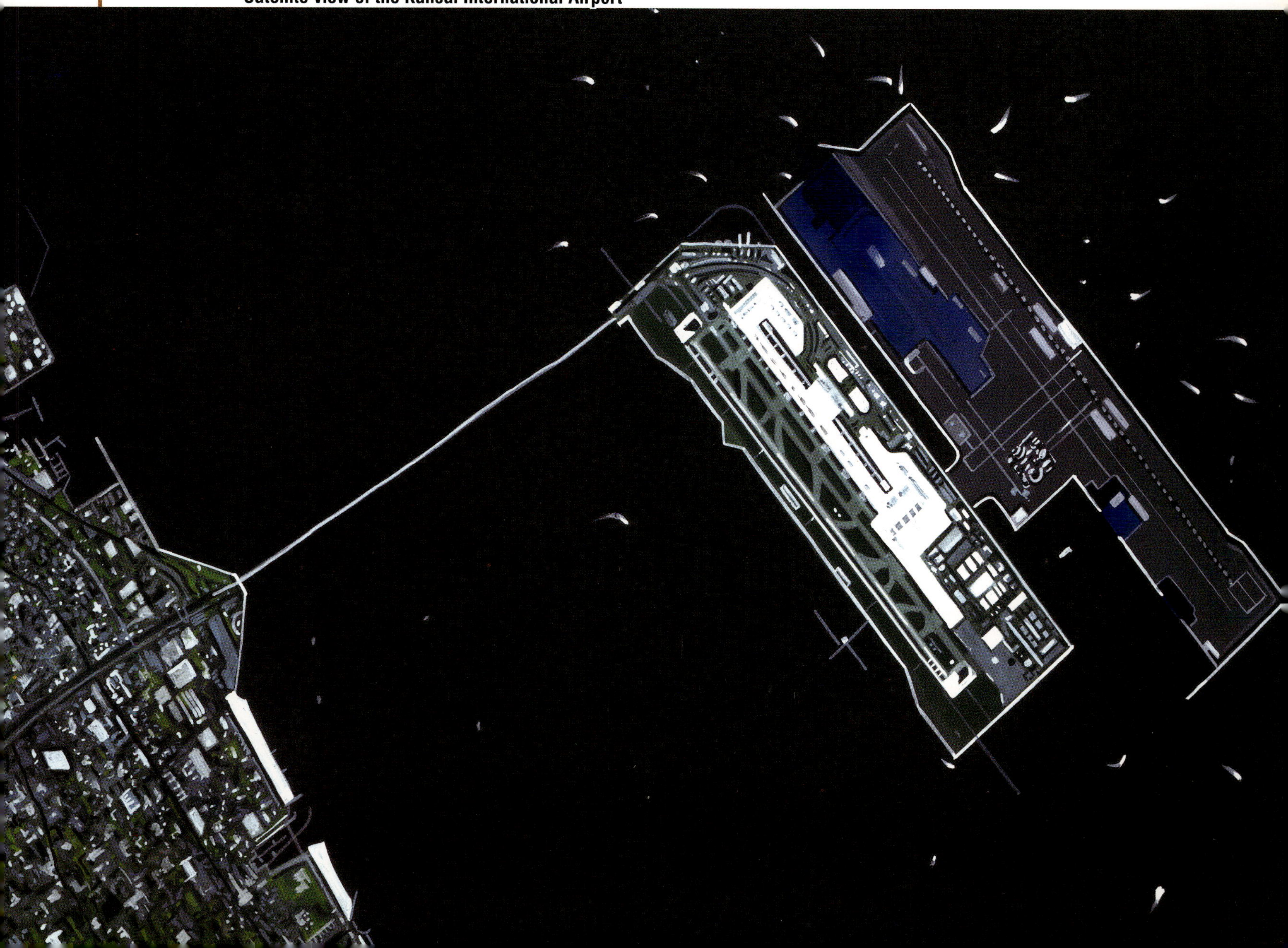

Terminal building of the Kansai International Airport

Terminal

The Kansai International Airport has a single four-story terminal. The terminal is 1.6 km long and is the longest terminal in the world. It was designed by an Italian architect Renzo Piano. The terminal is an aluminium and glass frame structure with an airfoil-shaped roof. The arrivals are on the 1st floor while the departures are from the 4th floor. The terminal has an advanced people moving system, called the Wind Shuttle that is used to move people from one end of the piers to the other.

Renzo Piano

Renzo Piano was an Italian architect. He was born in Genoa, Italy in September 1937. Piano studied architecture at the University of Florence and at Milan Polytechnic. Piano is well-known for his museum designs. The Kansai International airport is his best known work.

Awards

Kansai airport was awarded "Monument of the Millennium" by the American Society of Civil Engineers. It also ranked 4th overall in the Airport of the Year 2006 awards named by a British research company, Skytrax.

Glossary

barge: A large, flat-bottomed boat built for river and canal transport of heavy goods.

canyon: A long, narrow valley with steep sides cut by running water.

cavea: The tiered sitting area of an ancient theatre, especially Roman theatre.

colonnade: A series of columns set at regular intervals for supporting a roof.

delta: A deposit of sand and soil usually triangular at the mouth of a river.

ebony: The hard, dark-coloured wood used for carving.

equinoxes: The time in the sky when sun crosses the equator.

Iguana: A large tropical American lizard that feed on insects and vegetation.

Ishtar Gate: The eighth gate to the inner city of Babylon.

lagoon: A small lake divided from the sea by sand or coral reef.

laterite: A red soil rich in oxides of iron and aluminium found in tropics and sub-tropics.

lintel: The horizontal beam or stone over an opening that carries the weight of the structure.

masonry: A structure or building built by a mason with materials such as bricks, tiles, stones etc.

meteorite: A meteor fallen to the surface of the Earth from outer surface.

moat: A deep, broad ditch usually filled with water that surrounds a castle.

mound: A heap of earth or sand built over a grave for protection.

opera: A play or theatrical presentation consisting of dramatic performance.

peninsula: A large land surrounded by water that connects two large bodies of land.

pharaoh: A title used to refer to the kings of ancient Egypt.

plaque: A thin, flat piece of metal or wood with a picture or design.

podium: An elevated platform that supports the base of a column.

pyramid: A huge structure with a flat square and sloping sides meeting at the top.

rapids: A section of the river with shallow water that moves very fast over rocks.

Rhodes: A Greek island located in the southwest Aegean Sea.

shovel: A tool made of iron sheet used for lifting and moving loose material such as coal, dirt or sand.

spire: A tall, conical structure on the top of a building.

strait: a narrow passage of water that connects two larger bodies of water.

Stucco: A fine or coarse plaster or cement used to cover exterior walls or surface.

symphony: a large musical work usually containing three or four movements.

Index